Photographs by
GIANCARLO GARDIN

Written by
GIULIANA BIANCHI

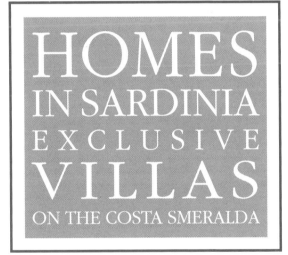

HOMES
IN SARDINIA
EXCLUSIVE
VILLAS
ON THE COSTA SMERALDA

English Translation by
JOAN RUNDO

Designed by
MAURIZIO PICCININI

ARCHIDEOS®
Books & CD

AURORAE CONSURGENTI
DICATUM EST
MCMXCIX

ARCHIDEOS

LIBRI & CD
CD & LIVRES
BOOKS & CD
CD & BÜCHER

ARCHIDEOS BOOKS
P.zza San Camillo de Lellis, 1 - 20124 Milano - Tel. +39 02 6698.4776 - Fax +39 02 6698.1740
www.archideos.com - info@archideos.com

TABLE OF CONTENTS

Architecture with a tempo measured by arches, passages, steps and varying levels on the waters of Porto Cervo.

A panoramic view of Porto Cervo
as imagined in a 1962 watercolour
by the architect Michele Busiri Vici.
An ingenious and intuitive designer, in this splendid sketch
he anticipated the architecture which he would to bring to life
in "Sa Conca, S'Abba Ilde, Sas Pedras, the Hotel Luci di La Muntagna"
and the "Stella Maris" church as well as individual villas and houses.
He designed "Sa Conca", his first work in Porto Cervo
(we can see views of on the following double page),
together with his son Giancarlo in 1963:
"...the linear and flowing continuity of the architecture at road level
with a tempo measured by arches, passages, steps
and varying levels that opens and reveals to visitors
and passers-by glimpses of rare beauty
on the waters of Porto Cervo..."

Giancarlo Gardin

My passion is photography; photography of homes and gardens, trying to describe, in images, the stories they have to tell. Initially I decide how to build up a visual journey through the internal and external rooms. Detail and views are integral to this journey together with photographic skills and techniques. Owners and designers work in harmony at the outset of each project.

The story is different every time, from the minor anecdotes at the beginning and the time of photographic narration lasts not only from dawn to dusk, but at times extends for days. But the real story, which only those who have seen me taking photographs, is that I use special cameras I have created and built specially. They now have a definite identity; called "Free Eye", they are produced and marketed for both amateur and professional photographers.

The book should therefore be seen from a dual point of view because it expresses a composite itinerary in contemporary architecture, limited to a specific place, the Gallura region, where there have been significant experiences in modern architecture, almost unique of their kind. I have been able to work there from the very beginning, covering twenty years of habitual visiting as photographer with an increasingly close relationship!

My first photographs of homes in Sardinia continue to be published; I consider them the supporting columns of a construction that has been completed in time, but which will never be really finished. Every time I take a photograph, I perceive the development that my work is

Giuliana Bianchi

Homes in Sardinia, exclusive villas on the Costa Smeralda.

Perhaps it is worthwhile dwelling on the title of this book which is perhaps more accurate than it may appear on first sight.

This book is about holiday homes in Sardinia, and more specifically on the Costa Smeralda. This name immediately evokes the boom of exclusive tourism in an uncontaminated spot, one of the most beautiful that exists. The aim of this volume is to see how and why these villas, designed by leading architects, have a reference value that is not only local but international.

A true architectonic body which is still unexplored as a whole and entitled to be seen not as the blossoming of a single work but as an interesting ensemble worthy of study, without fearing improper comparison from official critics. In contrast with a small group of contemporary coastal works which are fairly well known (for example the Villa Malaparte on Capri), there is an incessant demand for tourism-related building which has devastated landscapes because it has been left to anonymous architects whilst the best civil, professional

and intellectual forces have thought well of not dealing with this area. Our architects, on the other hand, starting from the pioneers such as Luigi Vietti, have pragmatically accepted a fact they did not oppose and have devoted their work to the configuration of both town-planning rules for a modern and sustainable development, and of suitable architectonic forms, to the extent of realizing interventions which are capable of leaving the quality of the environment intact.

The village of Porto Cervo is conceived in such a way as to reconcile the "culture of leisure" of the international holiday-making society with a new landscape for holidays. The works of the first creators on the Costa Smeralda, during the 1960s, which were authentically rooted in a tradition that was understood in depth and nevertheless courageous and inventive, have become, up to the 1990s, the examples which have inspired the architects we present in this book.

The sculpture-homes of Jacques and Savin Couëlle, the Mediterranean constructions of Michele Busiri Vici, the rationalist architecture of Vietti and Gamondi, Gérard Béthoux and Vanni Fiori contribute towards creating a landscape that is indeed constructed but where the scars of the earth have been tended to with particular care and attention. The height of the houses has been studied according to the flora. Indeed, as Luigi Vietti says in his interview, "the trees were small junipers… the change of proportion gave me the idea of building houses that could not be seen". Or as Marina Perrot, who followed Savin Couëlle on the building sites said: "when the plan of a house ended up against a tree, Savin altered the design not to sacrifice it".

What is surprising in all of them (both those who are absent from this book and those who are present) is that, in their architecture, mainly considered only "ephemeral" by "official" criticism, they all propose a figure that is both classic and innovative at the same time: the superintendent of beauty, the chief engineer, the curator of the territory and who, according recently passed laws, should exist in the technical department of all local authorities, but who does not exist.

As architecture and especially residential architecture, is a whole that evolves in time, the aim in this book has been to capture them at the height of their splendour through the evocative interpretation of Giancarlo Gardin's special camera. Designed on commission, as you will read in all the architects' accounts, it is only fair that the villas express in images the ultimate purpose for which they have been built.

Similarly, the interviews which I did exclusively for this book aim to give first-hand testimony of the intentions, designs, ideas and memories of some of the protagonists of this adventure.

Sardinia, an Island of Mistery

Sardinia, which Sardinia? The Sardinia of the eastern coast or of the western coast? The Sardinia that from the Gallura region extends to the beaches of the Maddalena archipelago or the Sardinia of the lunar dunes of Piscinas? The Sardinia of Carloforte, colonized by the Genoese or the Sardinia of Alghero, which was a Catalan military stronghold? This island has so many different faces, all different one from the other, that it would seem impossible at first sight to put them all together. "There is nothing in Italy that is in Sardinia and in Sardinia there is nothing that is in Italy" wrote Francesco Setti, a professor of mathematics sent to the University of Cagliari, when he arrived in 1774. And the diversity of Sardinia continues up to the present to be one of the specific features of this island which, 200 miles from the Italian coast, is still a land apart and as impenetrable as it is fascinating. Travellers should not be under any illusion: this is an extraordinary and mysterious place but also one that is hard to understand. All this is written in its history, related by its population and in its anecdotes. A journey back in time can tell us that when he arrived on the island Dante not very pleasantly labelled it a land of brothels and Honoré de Balzac, a few centuries later, was the victim of cheats whilst he was in search of fortune and silver mines and fled only two months after landing, to return to

Marseilles. Nor did he pretty up the image of Sardinia in his letters. Like Dante, he defined it a den of swindlers and bloodsuckers. Little does it matter that his business partner was a merchant from Liguria. But the halo of mystery surrounding Sardinia is also present in the island's offspring: one for all, Sebastiano Satta, considered the greatest Sardinian poet in the vulgate, has ambivalent feelings. Whilst enamoured of his land, he cannot help but mention the vendettas and bandits that have contributed to no small extent to the image of Sardinia. The mystery continues. And for this reason, talking about Sardinia is like trying to penetrate a mystery that envelopes this land from the beaches of Chia, east of Cagliari to the far north of Capo Testa. Nor is it a coincidence that Sardinia has never sold its soul to Mammon. If anything, it has sold part of its coasts: Sardinian pride has never let anyone colonize this island. And perhaps to realize why, it is sufficient to go just a few kilometres inland from the strobe lights of the discotheques and holiday complexes of the Costa Smeralda; along the road running between the cork tree groves of the Gallura to Tempio Pausania, the intense perfume of the Mediterranean maquis of a nature that has not yielded still fills the air. Here the air is fragrant with that combination of scents of lavender and lentisk, myrtle and juniper, arbutus and wild grass.

Alternatively, take the Carlo Felice, the highway that crosses the whole of Sardinia. Along this road, the name of which recalls the glories and great works of the Savoy kingdom on the island, the hardness and contradictions of the land can be seen but at the same time it reveals its fascination. Like Gabriele d'Annunzio, it is easy to fall in love with Sardinia, its low vegetation, its granite rocks, the mistral wind that blows across the whole of the northern

part: this strong and impressive nature which is the distinctive characteristic of the island. And it is precisely the relationship between nature and man that gives the landscape this harsh appearance. Sardinia, despite its more than 1,800 kilometres of coastline representing a quarter of the Italian coastal perimeter, essentially remains mountain country. And it is not so much the altitude of the Gennargentu, which is less than 2000 metres above sea level or the average altitude of the island that gives it this appearance. Its image comes from its traditions that are still very much alive and the local festivals which represent most of the social life in a land where the average population density is 69 per square kilometre and the more than seven thousand towers from the Nuraghic civilization standing guard over the valleys and the coasts. This condition of isolation in the island exists nowhere else in the Mediterranean, including Corsica. Because of its historic and environmental particularity and its extraordinary diversity, Sardinia has been defined one of the northern hemisphere's greatest open-air museums. Thus, the island's fundamental characteristics have been marked by the sea, the mountains, its isolation and the hardness of the granite of

its origins. Because, if it is true that Sardinia emerged over 500 million years ago as incandescent magma which cooled down in granite rock clusters, it was with this same granite that the Nuraghic civilization first, followed by all

the populations that came afterwards, built up their fortune. If the Nuraghi and the megalithic circles of the large collective burial grounds are one of the first forms of prehistoric architecture in the Mediterranean, granite still represents a natural wealth which cannot be left out of consideration for the whole of Sardinia. Evidence of this lies in the columns of the Pantheon in Rome and the use of granite during the Renaissance. In more recent times, Sardinian granite has become one of the most profitable items in the Sardinian economy. It has been used from Australia, on the facing of the Riverside Center in Brisbane, to New York, as well as Japan and this stone, with its absolute value, is also used for interior decoration. Granite has therefore become a fundamental element for any architectural work in Sardinia. There are two main reasons for this: the respect for a land which, although having

a thousand contradictions, has wanted to and succeeded in some way in maintaining its strong and different identity and, in the second place, because it is an element of prestige and beauty that must be the constant of any intervention by man on nature. Because as Vico Mossa says in "Architettura e paesaggio in Sardegna", "The relationship between architecture and landscape is the same as that between civilization and nature; and so the right rhythm has to be found, in virtue of which, consciously or unconsciously, those cultural assets which are the result of past civilizations have accumulated". And if building in the past cannot fully be considered architecture, it has to be recognized that the characteristics of humility, taste and craftsmanship of the majority of these constructions have not offended the surrounding environment. This is why the value of human intervention in architecture lies above all in the modesty of forms and the quietness of tone. A modesty that is far removed from the opacity and lack of colour to enhance the surrounding environment. Because in such a vibrant and intense land, intervention must be harmonious and never appear to invade the environment.

Above: 1964: Luigi Vietti
presents the first part
of the "Le Cerbiatte" village in Porto Cervo
to the Regional Council.
Below: view of the "Cala di Volpe" Hotel
on completion of the first construction.

Between rationalism and organic architecture

A doorway in one of Milan's most elegant streets, Corso Venezia; Luigi Vietti's study is in a period building and the working rooms are clearly separated from the studio.

The furniture is antique, the many windows are as high as the ceiling and look on to a lush internal garden, which cannot be seen from the outside, as is so often the case in the centre of this wealthy city. A quarter of an hour wait for the appointment in mid-afternoon. Some apprehension at the idea of interviewing the maestro who is now more than ninety years old. The walls are lined with books and pictures, including a beautiful portrait he himself did of his mother, one by Morlotti and a gouache by Guttuso. The desk has been replaced by a refectory table, the chairs are seventeenth-century, with a high back and ruby red velvet upholstery. That he is an architect of international renown can be seen from the "honorary citizenships of Portofino and Cortina", where he worked on town-planning, hanging on the walls and a drawing table, almost a piece of modern design, left neglected in a corner... The maestro does not need it; as he slyly admitted, he has a golden touch with a pencil!

Giuliana Bianchi: As well as designing individual villas, you have also worked on the town planning regulations of such marvellous places as Portofino, Cortina d'Ampezzo and the Costa Smeralda. Can you tell me something of your different experiences in two places which were inhabited and built up (and where it was a question of their preservation) and another place, Sardinia, where there was nothing.

Luigi Vietti: The impression that I had of Sardinia was that of proportion: there were no plants, no trees. There were rocks, sea and sky. The trees were small junipers, low but a hundred years old, and so their shape was that of an old tree. Seeing them from afar, they looked like a forest, but when a man with his cows passed by (because then there were cows grazing there) they looked twice as big as natural. This is the phenomenon that impressed me most of all. This sort of change in proportion gave me the idea of building houses that could not be seen. If you can see them too well, they become enormous compared to the landscape. The landscape was varied because there were the rocks and the conformation of the land; it was not perfectly flat but always undulated. What's more, this very old vegetation, with its complete formation but very low, not more than two and a half metres high, fitted into this landscape. I built a house close to a group of this type: since 1965, the trees have grown by perhaps 20 centimetres... In actual fact only one has grown, a juniper. I was very fond of this juniper, I made it a small courtyard. I built houses with not more than one floor, plus an upper floor (two floors in all), except with the complexes, where the complex allowed building something taller. I would say that these complexes were speculative in nature, searching for a correspondence of interest on the capital. I began to build there on two floors at the most, in order to try not to affect the landscape. That's not all. The Hotel Pitrizza was built completely camouflaged: the ground floor is low, made of rocks with bushes all around, the roof is a lawn (originally it was a garden with flowers, now it has become a lawn: apparently because it was impossible to find a gardener who looked after roofs...). This was one of the first camouflaged buildings, in other words that you can't see from above or from below or from the sea. Even the swimming pool was camouflaged. With a very thin edge, so that the seawater overflows and it is difficult to distinguish it from the water of the swimming pool. I dug out the rocks, which were brown and then I painted them pale blue and then a darker shade of blue, to give a sense of depth. This idea of having a swimming pool in the rocks conceals the work of man with regard to the work of nature. This is the principles of all my houses there. Then gradually, houses began to be built according to the client's requirements.

G.B.: That was true and original architecture. The client had to appreciate and believe in the work of his architect.

L.V.: I have always tried to have first class clients, who were cultivated and sensitive enough to accept my thinking, which at that time was somewhat different from normal. They were ideas difficult to understand straight away. And then there were other elements, such as the wind which at times blows at over 100 kilometres an hour. The window and door frames have to be solid. I invented a type of frame that was sliding and became compressed, a bit like a porthole made of wood and rubber. Then you had to deal with the conformation of the land. On rocky land, you have to build in such a way that the different floors are not added to one another. If you build several houses (even if they only have a ground floor and a first floor) on a slope without leaving any greenery between the first house and the second one, they form a skyscraper, with all the floors on top of each other. By respecting space, the perspective conceals each house in the other.

G.B.: How many villas do you remember having designed, more or less. And in how long?

L.V.: They're always asking me that but I don't know. In the region of a few dozen. When we designed Porto Cervo, we felt the need to make the residential part, because that was the commercial part. And so we built a group of seven houses which we called the "Romazzine", after the name of the place where we built them, one next to the other, like villas. We built them all at our risk but they were all sold without any transformations. They were villas with only a ground floor, separated by a small alley, three - three and a half metres wide, where there were no windows because the surfaces with windows had to be at least ten metres away. Then there was the front door and a small window to give light to the entrance. All these houses were linked and were very successful, so much so that one was bought by the Aga Khan.

G.B.: This typology of the "Romazzine" is one that you invented after the experience of seeing other things. In general, the architect seeks a source of inspiration on the spot but here, on the other hand, I think there are elements that come from journeys to far-off lands, from Portofino, from the Kasbah. I also think that the search for materials is affected by this type of inspiration as well. But an architect also has to take his client into account.

L.V.: I always design made to measure homes. If I don't know the person I have to build the house for, then I don't do it. I am stimulated by the client's demands. I have to know who they are, how they express themselves and what they do. Logically, if they have children or not. Then I build the house for them. If the person has a varied and agitated temperament, then the house is "varied..." The person in this case needs to have something that will always strike and surprise them. These houses are simple because there is only one floor that moves. For example, when I built my house, instead of a corridor I designed a bower. I am a fairly calm person but I am interested in houses. Normally I build vertical fireplaces but in my house I put a horizontal one. And I put my collection of antique sailing boats on it. I don't have any children but I have nephews and nieces. So I built a "house" for each of them. My niece is a brunette so I made her small apartment pink. My nephew is blond, so I did his green. I love this house and I still like it very much.

G.B.: Can you think of a job for one client in particular?

L.V.: The house for Princess Alexandra of Kent. The land was rocky, so I built a house with three levels. In one there is the reception part and two guest rooms. Then I did one level with the swimming pool, and the third with their apartments near the sea and the landing stage. The house is dynamic, with a bower connecting the three parts and is great fun and very pleasant.

G.B.: I've noticed that you pay special attention to the intersection between interiors and exteriors.

L.V.: In this house, the arrangement of the interior and exterior is the same. There is a divan and armchairs inside and a divan and armchairs outside. The outdoor ones are under an awning which can be pulled when there is the sun. The indoor and outdoor parts communicate with one another, it's a very affectionate house.

G.B.: What is your cultural matrix?

L.V.: I was born out of rationalism. Then the war came and, thinking about it, I came to the conclusion that the rationalistic elements created until then could always be repeated. So I said to myself that there were other forms that were still rational and that could be accepted. Poor architecture, the architecture of peasants or fishermen, which I had already studied. For my degree, I researched old peasant homes and I found an enormous amount of interesting solutions from the architectural point of view. I saved my rationalistic belief with elements that were different from those of official rationalism. I discovered a different world.

G.B.: How must an architect's work fit into the territory?

L.V.: I think that the architect who has to fit into the landscape has to understand it first of all. I would say that he has to submit to the landscape. He can manipulate it and change it with the presence of constructions: think of towers. forts, bunkers. The Austro-Hungarian constructions of the nineteenth century were so absolute that they imposed themselves on the landscape. Sometimes I took the risk of inserting something that was different compared to the morphology, precisely for the intention of forcing the landscape with my presence. For example, Villa Wanda in Stresa is an element in itself compared to the landscape. But it has been built with elements that I would call natural, without concrete (only the horizontal parts are in concrete). All the vertical walls are made of natural elements. In Sardinia I invented monoliths: I cut the rocks and I made pilasters of granite instead of concrete. This was to insert something natural. The horizontal parts have to be made of statically resistant elements: either I have an arch or I use wooden beams. Wooden beams in Sardinia were perhaps too "rustic" and so I used brickwork for the horizontal part. The Hotel Pitrizza and my house have the vertical parts with elements built by nature rather than by man. These materials give an emotion and a liveable and human architecture.

G.B.: I would like to talk about the Hotel in Cala di Volpe: what do you think of what Jacques Couëlle did?

L.V.: I found it a very courageous building because he succeeded, with the ideas of old constructions such as fortifications, in building something tall. It was not born as a hotel but as a restaurant with an apartment for the Aga Khan. So there was this apartment with a staircase going up to where the various rooms were with a bigger one for the prince. It was a success and so instead of seven rooms, they built twenty and then eighty and then a hundred.

The new hotel is very imaginative, as was Jacques Couëlle. He was not an architect. Nor was Le Corbusier an architect. Couëlle was a painter and so what he does is always pictorial. Clever and intelligent. It is an interesting work, also because he gave movement to the rigidity of the walls. He accepted making all the walls crooked (which I was already doing), all made by hand.

G.B.: Were you strongly influenced by your clients?

L.V.: I have built complexes, towards Liscia di Vacca, which were greatly transformed by an "impresario". They could have been very beautiful complexes but I didn't even recognize them. The first things I did for this person were sold straight away, again in Liscia di Vacca. So he could be certain of their marketability. But he changed my designs. These are professional disappointments. These apartments were sold at crazy prices with my name. I still build in Sardinia, but the municipal authorities no longer approve anything. I have a complex of 34 houses in a very interesting place; we have been waiting for permission for years. In the area where according to their plans you could build, trees have grown in the course of the years. And I refuse to build there; I would build close by, on the rocks but they won't let me because it doesn't come under that plan.

G.B.: Precisely for this reason, I would like to write about how you have transformed this Sardinia: with respect and sensitivity.

L.V.: Unfortunately not all operators are honest. As far as I'm concerned, people who destroy the landscape are criminals.

G.B.: Do you draw or make sketches when you get the first idea?

L.V.: I do all the rough work. My expert assistants do the executive part under my supervision. If you don't create from the beginning then you don't get anywhere, in the end there is nothing that is right.

G.B.: Supervision is everything then. Like all great architects, you can draw well.

L.V.: Of course I can draw well!

GIANNI GAMONDI

Villas... the evolution of the Holiday Village

A quiet apartment in the streets near Milan's Central Station. Nothing too ostentatious. Technology appears discreetly in the reception and in the offices of his assistants, but not where we are met. Gianni Gamondi does not like computers and feels that he belongs to the generation in the middle: he puts the idea down on paper and when he needs to go into it in greater detail or check it, he turns to one of his assistants. He loves the Costa Smeralda and as well as being an angler he also plays golf. We talk to him one morning at nine. He is an early riser, has blue eyes, a sportsman's build and we deduce his age from the fact that he graduated from Milan's Politecnico the same year as Renzo Piano... Thirty years of architecture flow from his lips. His commissions, from the most complex to the simplest, become the yardstick against which he measures, with remarkable modesty, everything he has done. There is still a great deal to do on the other side of the ocean, in unknown islands where, seven years ago, he began the great adventure of the Club K on Barbuda with fashion designer Krizia; this success will perhaps take him far from Sardinia and which, earlier still, together with his then partner Vittorio Antonioli, he had already marked out in Brazil with Luigi and Nicolò Donà delle Rose.

Giuliana Bianchi: What professional experience have you gained in Sardinia?

Gianni Gamondi: On the Costa Smeralda I learnt that "something" that was of use in my professional life, for other designs. The Costa Smeralda makes you think, it sets queries and asks the reasons for "certain" solutions. Then you make your choice, maybe different, but in the meantime this land has led you to reason, something that before was not done, not even at university. Also because then at university tourism did not exist, at the most there were "London's satellite towns"...

G.B.: We can say that town planning for holidays does not exist. Except in some towns in America, where there are affluent pensioners and where some more planning has been done regarding retirement.

G.G.: What I have greatly appreciated was the town planning of the Costa Smeralda. The urban design on a virgin territory, the fact of having developed a plan. A fabric of "mini urban furnishing" was woven. This had never happened before, it was not done at all. The type of architecture led me to reflect on what were certainly my points of view. I elaborated a "style" of my own (let's call it that) even if personally I am against the idea of "style" in architecture: it is only the evolution of taste, "fashion".

G.B.: When you were very young and began to design these things, who was your myth, your master?

G.G.: Alvar Aalto. There is a strong element of rationality in his works. Aalto is the only person who combines rationality and a very precise function with a minimum of emotion. Like Frank Lloyd Wright, even if he was more "fashionable".

G.B.: Moreover, Alvar Aalto was inspired by Wright and had filtered him through his own culture. I won't ask you if you like Le Corbusier, Mr. Gamondi...

G.G.: "Style" must be a way of putting a halt on certain codifying that may take root and become the end and no longer the means to attain "something" in architecture. When a style becomes too binding, then the Le Corbusiers who break away, or even the Brutalists, who bring concrete, are fine. But then you have to return to emotion, as you were saying; you need that as well. The absolute does not exist and each subject is something new. The nice thing about my work is just that. You are not pre-packed.

G.B.: I recognize the Gamondi style, if I can put it that way, because it is clean, Italian and essential. Even in Sardinia, it can be clearly distinguished from others.

G.G.: At times the professionals influences the client one hundred per cent, the guest of the work being done. I give value, initially, precisely to the function, but it must not be an end in itself. It is not the function that must become the rule. The function is the rule for the correct specification: "the car is for", "the house is for" and "the factory is for...". If the architect has a predominant relationship with the client, then a sort of reverential fear of the client may be born for the master who, as such, cannot be touched.

G.B.: You build everywhere. Don't you have a particular *genius loci?*

G.G.: Territory is not a blank page. For me it is a problem to be solved. I have lived with difficult, rocky and uneven land prone to landslides all my life and that is what gives me the greatest stimulus. On flat ground you build a house and next to it there is another and you cannot see it, it disappears. When you go into the hills it's different. Like the house of Philippe Leroy, the first I built on the hill behind Porto Rotondo. When we put up the first scaffolding two and a half metres high (because we had to use the scaffolding not to touch the rocks) I saw that those gigantic oaks were in actual fact trees two metres twenty high and I had to scale down all the ratios, the dimensions and the colours. In Sardinia the proportions are like bonsai: junipers reach a maximum of three metres. I remember the words of Andrea Cascella, who I worked with when we were building the church of Porto Rotondo (I also worked with Pietro for a villa in Sardinia). I expressed my doubts as a young architect from the rationalist school who was coming to build houses on the Costa Smeralda straight after leaving the Politecnico in Milan. And he said a very fine thing to me which was of great help to me and which goes like this: "Compromise is not a nice thing but life is made of compromises. Never go beyond the moral limit. You are often influenced by the client. You always put something of yours in houses, then even if the house as a whole is not only yours, that little piece is your expression and your acquisition". Very often I give in to the clients but I also have to deal with problems that depend on town-planning regulations. Sometimes I'm able to overcome the influence and express myself, even if all the rest is standard with little or nothing in terms of enrichment of my professional life.

G.B.: I would like to highlight some elements of your architecture: your love for nature, shown when you cut floors to save a small plant of myrtle.

G.G.: The respect for the landscape leads to the enhancement of the territory. And it is here that you really feel that you are facing up to nature. You really feel a nature like Sardinian nature and it is a challenge not to destroy it but to enhance it.

G.B.: Another strong element is functionality. Explain how you decide the layout, in relation to the your clients needs.

G.G.: You have to be something of a psychologist with your clients, you have to understand how they live and know how many pairs of shoes they have... I place great importance on the kitchen and the bathroom, especially in Sardinia where the bathroom is used a lot. You take several showers a day and you have time to enjoy this room; in addition, the bathroom depends on the bedroom; sometimes we have had two bathrooms for the same bedroom, precisely to satisfy the client's requirements and for a question of functionality. The kitchen is the other space where you can express yourself. Some of my houses have enormous kitchens. A house, like clothes, must respond well.

G.B.: In the houses you own what is paramount, the beauty, utility or the client's comfort?

G.G.: In the first place I own the land on which it is built: someone who wants a house in Sardinia wants to see outside. My Country Village in Porto Rotondo is the epitome of privacy, no two terraces are at the same level. Each terrace has to have a view and must be conceived with a total function. This is the first point of morality regarding the client: he buys an apartment and must have the maximum benefit, at least the view! Then comes functionality. Yesterday I was able to design a small apartment with 52 square metres, excluding the walls, and to sleep eight people? an apartment that was almost a challenge. These seem aberrations, but where there is a study with high costs (both for who is building and who is using the house), it seems only fair to me. Only later can there be fun, with the ladder that strains your legs. Jacques Couëlle has conceived architecture as fluids, or entrails: organic architecture. It is my conviction that you can "dress up" a part of the clientele. The others accept but they are slightly forced. When a detail in a house satisfies the creativity of the architect, the client can enjoy it calmly; but when the solutions that have been adopted are not very functional then their hand is being forced a bit too much. I always try to make the house liveable. Of course, I give myself little treats now and again as well.

G.B.: What inspires you as an architect? The fireplace, the window overlooking the sea...

G.G.: My houses can always be recognized by the view: enjoying the exterior from the interior. From the very first sketch I always realize that I immediately see the windows, the parts with a perspective. Then the living areas which are never forced and never contrived. I like open space in the day area: the dining room, the lounge... and the fireplace must be completely fluid... Usually the kitchen is separate but that depends on the client. I can make the kitchen a real "machine" for eating, but I have also designed enormous kitchens, where the kitchen looked like an ordinary kitchen with a dishwasher and oven, whilst it is almost an industrial kitchen with huge pans for feasts!

acquiring, especially for the place where I have gone. For this reason, I like going to the same places and meeting the same people: they will then be the ones to take me to others I had not met before.

However, the book also relates a very original technical experiment of mine, the "Free Eye", my invention in photography.

In 1988, following a personal intuition, thanks to the collaboration with an ingenious and refined mechanical engineer, I developed the first prototype of the "Free Eye", in a metal alloy which is normally used in aeronautics. Now it is a real tool of work which looks like a small disc and is mounted between the lens and the body of the photographer's camera, to obtain, with outstanding simplicity and rapidity, all the optical movements necessary to correct, both the perspective and the falling lines of each photograph, and in particular if they are of geometric subjects. In architecture, we know that each building, each of its rooms and each piece of furniture in it are of a geometrical shape: thus without corrections, the geometrical shapes would always appear deformed or distorted, with very few exceptions. Before now, only professional photographers could correct this using large and studio "optical bench" cameras, or with lenses of the "decentralizing" type, which are expensive, cumbersome and not at all practical.

On the other hand, since then, all my work has been done with "Free Eye" and the photographs in this book are its most complete "testimony". In particular, thanks to its being extremely rapid to use, I have been able to become a reporter as well as a photographer, seizing with "correct" images that "glance" which captures a ray of light as it passes by a window and seeing a boat pass on the horizon!

All this is only thanks to an intuition: "just as your eye is free to move the pupil between the lids", so when you use a lens you can move it freely too, rotating it in the circle of its range, over the entire image!

This apparatus may also be applied, keeping the same identical characteristics, on to professional telecameras which can now have "camera movements" until now impossible.

Evocations that give a complete meaning to the moment as experienced, returning it in its entirety with the sense of time and succession of events which remain linked to it, being expressed whenever those images are proposed again: there is nothing magic nor technical but the alchemy of a set of factors which are connected to one another: I have simply applied the possibilities the technological element offered me to relate to my method of expression.

I hope that it will be the same thing for you with my Free Eye.

G.B.: We are talking about very wealthy clients.

G.G.: The client who is not wealthy is the one with the 52 square metre apartment which is divided into two so that the children can fit in. But making such a small house work is a satisfaction for an architect. Cost has only a fifty per cent, never a hundred per cent influence, on building a beautiful house. The limit of a small budget also has a 50 per cent influence on me. The other half depends on my ability to interpret and make something beautiful with only those resources. Sometimes having unlimited means becomes a limit: being able to work without limits of cost may lead to deformations and excesses...

G.B.: How do you blend local traditions with your plans?

G.G.: Local traditions have their reasons. Sardinia has its materials, its granites and its ceramics: very fine and special products which are true art. I have almost always only used local materials. There were the tiles, the clay pantiles. I salvage them because they have a wonderful patina and immediately give a marvellous colour. But underneath I put new pantiles. For the Sporting Club, with Sandro Pianon, we used new tiles and at a certain moment that red was too noticeable so we called the people from Cinecittà to find out how to give them an antique look: a fellow made us pour pots of broth over them: the broth immediately forms a mould on top but in time it wears off...

G.B.: Do you use juniper beams?

G.G.: It's illegal to use them now. But I have hardly ever used them.

G.B.: And so apart from granite, what other Sardinian materials are there?

G.G.: The ceramics from Cerasarda, the stones on the ground. On the other hand, the pantiles come from Florence. But there is the vegetation. If you can help the local vegetation by giving it some water in July and August, it grows very lushly. But you have to be careful because too much water kills the juniper but not the olive tree which grows. The arbutus becomes a huge full plant, naturally as long as it has room. Sardinia has very fine essences...

G.B.: Is the ideal house a holiday home?

G.G.: In the house where you live, functionality and the norm have to be privileged but in a holiday home even a crazy idea is possible, even for the client and even in the small apartment of 52 square metres a bit of craziness is accepted.

G.B.: What is your relationship with Sardinia?

G.G.: It is a love-hate relationship. Recently the policy of the local authorities has been to deny any form of town planning and unauthorized building has been fuelled that way. We've been waiting for the so-called "master plan" in Porto Cervo for 25 years. It's ridiculous. And then the disgusting thing emerges and a territory is killed off. I go to Sardinia almost every week and when I arrive in the summer I find it distorted, I can't even see nature and there are too many crowds. It is not a place that can absorb all the people that arrive.

G.B.: And what about the building of Porto Rotondo?

G.G.: Vietti, the Couëlles, De Marchi, and Busiri Vici worked in Porto Cervo. There was great competition amongst them. I settled down in Porto Rotondo and I began there with the Counts Donà delle Rose, clients, and their entourages: the architect Sandro Pianon. Then I worked with my then partner, Vittorio Antonioli, everywhere, in the areas where there was not this struggle: Porto S. Paolo, Coda Cavallo, Puntaldia. I have never had any competitors. Porto Cervo was created one or two years before Proto Rotondo and I remember that we would watch each other during the works. Porto Cervo must date back to 1965 or 1966. I am sure that in 1967 Cala dei Volpe had not yet been built.

G.B.: Did you design the square in Porto Rotondo?

G.G.: I designed the Hotel San Marco. When I arrived there were already Pianon's first two houses. I did the arcades with the columns and the San Marco behind them and then I continued with the houses. Ninety per cent of Porto Rotondo is mine as well. I imagined a kasbah with narrow winding streets and low houses. In my opinion, if that complex could have been built with 10 thousand cubic metres instead of 12 thousand it would have come out better, I would have removed some parts that did not completely convince me. But the client (and by the way we were friends) had to cover the expenses!

G.B.: However, it is an example.

G.G.: My firm was the first to make official lots in Sardinia. I remember that at Coda Cavallo I convinced a client to build on only 13 per cent of the territory. A very nice person and a good friend, but it was difficult to get him to understand that I was giving him 13 per cent to build on and the rest would remain greenery. But when we finished it, he was fair: he said we were right. However, a change of law stated that all new buildings have to be 300m from the sea, I had to cut the terraces from the design so that the accomodation would fit in and so there are houses with lawns on the roofs and some roofs have become the garden of the complex.

G.B.: You have understood the most profitable purpose: the surrounding nature. There are professions in which you have to really understand your interest; ruining a place is not worthwhile either... it's better to keep it in a good condition.

G.G.: You have understood the philosophy of the inclusion of summer tourism.

G.B.: Let's talk about the so-called architectural falsity of the tourist marina, Port-Grimaud, "la petite Venise" for example.

G.G.: I see architectural falsity within the limits of composition. Pure falsity is one thing whilst the design detail of the house, at times, has to be pulled out with some detail or another.

G.B.: An architectural language with Italian roots seems evident to me here.

G.G.: In Sardinia I have used the three-centred arch: this is the architecture of Lombardy, the farmhouse, the spinning mill... there is hardly ever the Venetian or Roman arch. The three-centred arch is something that comes specifically from my Lombardy and certainly not from Sardinia. It is modest and at the same time you have to relate it to the local dimensions. If I were to design a Roman arch in Sardinia!

G.B.: You are working in the Caribbean now. What materials are you using?

G.G.: Wood from Canada and very light structures that come from the British tradition. Such a radical change is a stimulus and a new challenge.

GIUSEPPE CARTERI

The experience in the Costa Smeralda's gardens

Thirty-four years in Sardinia have not dampened Giuseppe Carteri's enthusiasm for his activity which I would like to underline by a neologism, landscape manager. Once again, in this study of the villas of the Costa Smeralda, *Falling Water* by Frank Lloyd Wright, came into my mind as a benchmark. This house, the protagonist of a famous film by Alfred Hitchcock with Cary Grant, with its audacious geometrical forms and natural materials such as wood and stone, dominates the landscape with its horizontal lines and simple forces with no frills. In this part of Sardinia with its straightforward materials and the contrast between the buildings and surrounding vegetation, it has been essential for the skill of the architects to have at their sides a trusty collaborator to find solutions that could heal the scars left by the sites. As a practical and farsighted man, Carteri has become a key person and thanks to him, Sgaravatti Mediterranea has designed the most beautiful gardens on the Costa Smeralda. "Good building" and the garden, may I suggest paraphrasing Wright, "have to make the landscape better than it was before". With Carteri, our architects have done just that.

Giuliana Bianchi: You are from Padua. What made you come to Sardinia?

Giuseppe Carteri.: I worked for Sgaravatti which is a Padua-based company. In 1963 they had signed an agreement with the Aga Khan to landscape the Costa Smeralda. There was already a branch in Cagliari and we followed the beginning of the development of the Costa Smeralda from Cagliari. Then the owners of the Hotel Romazzino, through the architect Michele Busiri Vici, commissioned a series of works from us to design the garden and so the Porto Cervo branch was opened in 1978. We began to work with the architects.

G.B.: Are there differences between the architects as far as landscaping is concerned?

G.C.: Sensitivity and choices are different, but they have the same ideas: restore nature where it has been damaged by the building sites: as few lawns as possible. Lawns cost less than Mediterranean maquis because myrtle and arbutus grow much more slowly. And so for an "immediate effect" there are oases of lawns with oaks and olive trees. At first, we ran into many difficulties because there was no water. But if you think that watering solves the problem, then you discover that in fact the problem is quite the contrary. You can save a lot of water by proper fertilization, with the right soil and with the right holes. But the soil in Sardinia does not retain anything. What it gets drains away. Abundance is immediately waste. Regular watering is essential. The soil is of granite origin.

For lawns we use Uganda, a special variety of grass. It has a problem: in the winter it hibernates, becomes yellow and seems dry. It turns green again towards mid-March. It is a ready-to-use carpet, which is rolled out after having been prepared in the nursery. In the spring it only needs a little attention.

G.B.: What can you tell us about the site?

G.C.: We are the last to arrive on the site: our time is very limited. The majority of the work is done in the summer, with enormous difficulties. We have acres of garden to finish by May. We are ready for the people who arrive here and want everything immediately. The people come on holiday and don't want any problems. We show them our material and in general there are no problems.

G.B.: Which elements do you take into consideration to landscape a garden on the Costa Smeralda?

G.C.: The majority of the plants have to flower in the summer, only a few people come at Easter, and so our organization aims at the summer. The lawn should be a minimum part, the majority is the *maquis* (mediterranean arboretum vegetation) and colours and scents.

As flowers I would choose hibiscus, plumbago and hydrangeas; we exclude azaleas and gardenias because the soil isn't suitable. Then the various types of rosemary, broom, arbutus and myrtle. Citrus trees, fig-trees, apricot and plum trees which are planted in the parts less exposed to the wind. Very few apples because they ripen in the wrong period and very few roses because they bloom in the spring. Then laurel trees and olive-trees. We have studied the olive tree and people love them, especially the trunks. The trunk of the olive tree is a sculpture... The olive tree, the holm-oak and the cork oak are three ancient trees that we plant in all gardens. There are very few palms because they are prohibited by the regulations of the Consortium of the Costa Smeralda, as are cypresses and pines. Every important villa has its four or five olive trees.

G.B.: What are the dimensions of a parcel of land for a villa with an impressive garden?

G.C.: Recently we have been in the

region of 6/7 thousand square metres. People want large gardens. The villas are now at their third or fourth owners and we can see that, unlike the past, the garden is very important. In fact, I work better now than before. Today, seriousness pays off. Consider that the garden helps to mask a lot of things, including the defects of the land. The garden increases the capital. The price varies according to whether you want a "ready-made" garden or a garden that grows slowly: the first is far more expensive. The best thing is directly showing the client the plants when he comes to choose them at the nursery.

G.B.: I've noticed that the swimming pools are far more integrated in the house today rather than in the garden.

G.C.: Today a villa at the sea means living outdoors. It is the outside that needs attention. People need space outdoors and want their privacy.

G.B.: What professional experience do you have?

G.C.: I graduated in agriculture and came to Sardinia at 22. It was a fantastic experience. I worked for the Aga Khan who was an exceptional man: he would go and visit the sites at five in the morning. The Costa Smeralda is thanks to him and his passion.

G.B.: In your opinion, what are the typical elements of Sardinian architecture?

G.C.: The shepherd's house, the "stazzu", in the Gallura region is very different from architecture in the Cagliari area. There is a great deal of Arabic culture in the south of Sardinia. The shepherd's house in Gallura is a sort of farmhouse, built of granite stone; a normal house with its fireplace, the kitchen garden outside and bedrooms, all in a rectangular shape. You go in, there is the large kitchen with its fireplace then there is the sleeping area. All on one floor. Here there is a certain culture in working with granite. It is difficult and needs accuracy; it is a skill that is handed down from father to son.

G.B.: I know that after some years you restructure your gardens: what are you pleased to change after 25 years on the Costa Smeralda?

G.C.: Today I try to bring the Mediterranean maquis as close as possible to the house and, at the same time, add colour. Whilst earlier we were oriented towards lawns, today we prefer Mediterranean maquis surrounded by colour. Today we use climbing plants, bougainvillaea, passionflower, honeysuckle, wisteria less because it flowers in the springtime, and plumbago. We try to mix as much as possible; we also look for the fragrance of jasmine and gardenia.

MARINA PERROT

A thesis on the Costa Smeralda

I meet her in the studio of our mutual friend and photographer Giancarlo Gardin. This tall lady with a very casual appearance has spent a lifetime on sites with her husband. She knows everything about Sardinia and in particular the Maddalena archipelago. They have had their firm Acquamarina in Sardinia since 1967. Their first job was to build the village of Porto Massimo with 65 apartments placed around a tiny harbour and a hotel with a capacity of 140 people. In the 1970s they specialized in various town planning studies of the Gallura region and have worked on several projects in the Consortium of the Costa Smeralda, such as Piccolo Pevero and Cala Corallina, north of Porto Cervo. Another area of activity was the Costa Paradiso, where they have built about thirty villas.

Giuliana Bianchi: What were your first impressions as a young architect when you arrived in Sardinia?

Marina Perrot: Houses in Gallura are very fine houses: tall and on two floors. Square, always with a balcony in the centre of the first floor. These were the houses of the gentry whilst the more modest lived in the "stazzu", where there was no comfort: a place to lay down, a stove, a table, two chairs and that was it. Twenty years ago a lot of people lived like that. I know a very nice little story. We had a piece of land after Santa Teresa looking west. The land was truly beautiful but very bleak and exposed to the mistral. Then the ravines were thick with vegetation and inaccessible whilst the upper parts were clipped by the wind. Once I went alone. Going backwards and forth from my land to the village I saw a "stazzu" and a woman. On my return I found another one with two women, a mother and her step-daughter. They were going to Santa Teresa to buy soap and perhaps coffee. They made their own butter, cheese and bread. They were self-sufficient five kilometres from Santa Teresa.

G.B.: What were these houses like inside?

M.P.: The rooms were bare. Two chairs, a dresser. They are beautiful because they are placed in very special positions, rather than the building in itself.

G.B.: I can hear great affection for the land in your words.

M.P.: I was fascinated by Sardinia. In my times, a young man would walk six kilometres to go and see his fiancée. For certain aspects you could say that I've almost caught "the African sickness".

G.B.: You arrived at a time when this island was still magical...

M.P.: Of course. It was the "Caribbean" and a forgotten archipelago. There was nobody there. The only harbour was in Porto Cervo, where there were about 30 boats. Large boats. And nature was unspoiled too.

G.B.: We're talking about thirty years ago. And now what does this island mean to you?

M.P.: I lived there when there was nothing. A sort of paradise. I tried to take part in the political life of La Maddalena which was in any case a particularly difficult area because the islanders, with the military arsenal, were used to being subjects of the State, not to do anything. So they developed the taste for grumbling and criticizing. I tried but I was disappointed. Gallura is different, there are a lot of people there who have acquired a certain economic affluence thanks to the Aga Khan and the development that followed.

VANNI FIORI

New clients and hidden technology

Vanni Fiori met me in Sardinia, at Olbia airport, one Saturday morning. We decided to speak about his designs on the way. "I began when I was very young, on site, following the works being built by Luigi Vietti", he tells me, "and I still follow some things for him. The maestro still comes occasionally, but he is very busy. Then I replace him". With great respect, I add. There is no-one who knows the detailed geography of the Costa Smeralda better than Vanni Fiori: every shrub and every stone. With commitment and a love for the traditions of his land (he is from here and likes to stay here) he combines efficient technology that is always well concealed with a search for ancient motives to propose in the interior decoration, from the designs of the corsets of the women's traditional costumes, to local carpets, the cane-woven porch roofs which, like a brise-soleil, are plentiful on his façades. Honest and shy, he comes to life when talking about the future of this splendid Coast. He fears unauthorized building and would like plots to reach one hectare per villa.

His pride and joy? Swimming pools. Sinuous and intriguing, with stones skimming the surface and jets of water, finishes of a sophisticated simplicity, at night they are illuminated with special effects, competing with the seawater for fascination and emerald transparency.

Giuliana Bianchi: I have noticed that you pay great attention to the interiors of the houses you build, following all the work, from the landscaping down to the last fabric. Your houses are also characterized by the Sardinian crafts in them...

Vanni Fiori: This is also due to the need for research; even for the fabrics I have gone to look for the details on Sardinian women's costumes, transferring them on to exclusively made tiles. The client likes this very much and so do I. I have departed somewhat from the path of my maestro, Luigi Vietti, seeking, especially in graffiti, with the collaboration of Cerasarda, a motive for research. Also because I would not want to build a typically Sardinian house which is, besides, very poor.

G.B.: As you are Sardinian, you know the typical Sardinian house very well. What is it like? I believe that in this area there was very little building...

V.F.: There were the shepherd's houses, the "stazzus" which are characterized by very simple elements or plastered stone (because the binder is almost always only clay or earth) or when a little more money was available, there was the rivalry to see who could make the richest and finest cornice on the front. These projections are very interesting, especially inland from the Costa Smeralda. Luogosanto, 20 kilometres from Arzachena, is a point of reference for me; I go there often, especially alone. There are some excellent houses there, often austere but in very good taste. That is where the really the typically Sardinian house with an abundance of granite is, rather than Olbia, because it is closer to the quarrying area. Despite the abundance of granite, quarrying has not been greatly developed along the coast, but much more inland: Luogosanto, Aggius, Luras. That type of classic and simple building can be found in those villages. The tiles finish at the edge; it is wholly a question of economics, there's not much else to say. I find Sardinian door and window frames very poor and essential. Obviously our parents tried to reduce to a minimum the space for the sun to penetrate. The arch certainly exists in Sardinian architecture. There is a very pretty village called Rizzo, famous for its nougat, where there are even public promenades with arches. The round arch exists, but so does the longitudinal arch. The three-centred arch, which Vietti uses, does not exist. I have to say that it was Vietti who imported them.

G.B.: What do you think of the town planning lay-out in Porto Cervo and Porto Rotondo?

V.F.: Porto Cervo is definitely better from the point of view of distribution of services. And size as well. It is also true that Porto Rotondo has grown out of proportion, unfortunately also with unauthorized building. And this unauthorized building has not been stopped. Whilst the Consortium of the Costa Smeralda has been concerned ever since the beginning (and today this is to its credit) by "absolute respect". On the sites, the guards of the consortium reached us before those of the municipal authorities.

G.B.: Who set up the Consortium?

V.F.: It was formed by a group of owners grouped together by the Aga Khan, who contributed with the land. This body was then set up to protect the territory. The majority belonged to the Aga Khan but there were other large owners, Fumagalli and Miller.

The consortium covers the 4 thousand hectares of the Costa Smeralda true and proper. The commune of Golfo Aranci, born 12 years ago, has 7 thousand hectares. The Costa Smeralda covers almost the same territory as a commune. About a third has been built up and occupied.

G.B.: It seems to me that the Costa Smeralda has always had the characteristic of Italian chic. Since 1965, we have gained a great deal of knowledge on holiday architecture and on holiday villages and villas of a certain type because we have measured ourselves up against the rest of the world. But you are the inventors of this style: I am talking about the pool of people who have worked here. You have wagered on a new architecture, which did not previously exist, that was suitable for this coast, which went well with the territory behind it and which was not totally without foundations. The materials, this whitewash and the deliberately poor tiles nevertheless recall our south and the Mediterranean basin.

V.F.: Research was done and this has to be acknowledged. There was also the desire to create a union between the old and the needs of today: naturally the sliding window did not exist in the shepherd's house. There has always been the same basic principle: maximum respect for the place.

G.B.: And so you see a possibility to go ahead: it is not a dead end.

V.F.: You have to think of the rhythm of modern life. And so you choose a whole range of materials that are practical to use. The individual handmade tile is of course beautiful, but it creates problems of maintenance in the cooking area... Compared to the past, there are no longer live-in staff and this causes a change in the lay-out of the interior of the house as

well. I have set myself the aim of reaching a union between marble, stone and tiles, And I think that the result is a good one. For example, transferring the pattern of the Sardinian carpet on to the tiles. It was greatly appreciated. Related with the bushhammered granite. Pleasant to the touch, easy to use and beautiful at the same time.

G.B.: I think that you pay particular attention to technology. Using air-conditioning rather than closing windows or insulation to make houses that avoid any traumas or problems for the stressed people who come here on holiday. And hiding all the technological parts very well. Everything that is needed is there but cannot be seen.

V.F.: I hate technology that can be seen. In Sardinia it would be a real eyesore and so I conceal it and put it in alcoves.

G.B.: Let's talk about clients and relationships with the client. Do you believe, like Luigi Vietti, that the client has to be a friend, someone who understands?

V.F.: Of course. Indeed, Vietti had his own way of dealing with the client in a very friendly way and had very few examples of difficult clients to deal with. I think that here he is well known especially for his calm temperament and his tranquillity. Sometimes I have wondered how he did not lose his temper with certain extremely demanding and at times capricious clients. I am the first to be helpful when the client is really interested in the problem and wants to obtain a result.

G.B.: The concept of practicality must never be forgotten. Both you and Vietti want the client to be happy in his home.

V.F.: The important thing is that there is a pattern of practicality right from the start. Vietti has always been recognized as building very practical homes. I think that when the client goes to Vietti he knows this.

G.B.: Which materials do you generally use on the Costa Smeralda?

V.F.: Canes for the bowers. Contrary to general belief, a bower that is treated well can last for up to 8 or 10 years. From the quality point of view, I use craftsmen who work almost only for me. The supporting wood is chestnut.

G.B.: And juniper?

V.F.: Juniper grows depending on how it is fed. I like it as a natural trunk. Not as planks because its veins are too rustic and irregular. Junipers are highly protected. You can find juniper that has been salvaged from fires. I like it for its perfume. If it is used for furniture, you can smell its perfume for a long time. In Sardinia it was traditionally used as a lintel above doors and windows and in rooms as the ridgepole, up to six metres long. There is also the flesh-coloured marble of Orosei. And field boulders, which are hewed by specialized local craftsmen.

G.B.: What future do you see for the Costa Smeralda?

V.F.: The Costa Smeralda is protected and continually checked: there is a continuous turnover of operators within the building trade. In 33 years, 1,200,000 cubic metres have been built. Now renovation and restructuring work is being done. Enlarging the parcels of land helps to protect the landscape by hiding the volumes in the greenery. I do not think that mass tourism can represent a possible future. It is pointless building another harbour in Cala di Volpe and another in Portisco. This territory must be preserved with the vocation for which it was created.

GÉRARD BÉTHOUX
Modern architecture that evokes the past

I met Gérard Béthoux one Sunday afternoon, in his refuge-studio, in a small house in San Pantaleo, a village behind the Costa Smeralda in the mountains, remarkably pointed and Dolomite-like, although on a miniature scale. The house, built of stone, has a central entrance hall which opens on to two rooms; the windows are tiny, the roof sloping, books, foreign and sophisticated magazines are mixed with tiles, terracotta and samples along the walls. Whilst we talk in the room on the left of the entrance, a large poster, showing an abbey, stares at me from the wall. This is where the interview starts and, under the influence of his words, Gérard shows me the pretty square of the village, filmed on many occasions, so remarkable it is in its cleanliness. Compared to the dimensions of Gérard, more or less like those of his famous homonym and fellow-countryman Dépardieu, the houses resemble a Christmas crèche scene like the square.

The poem by Aldo Palazzeschi, *Rio Bo,* comes to mind.

Giuliana Bianchi: How come a French architect came to Sardinia and has been working here for so many years?

Gérard Béthoux: I was born in Lyon, I studied in Grenoble for two years and then in Paris. My family is half from Grenoble and half from Lyon. I finished high school in 1968. The school of architecture in Lyon had been dismantled, it no longer existed. I went to Paris with other friends. In the meantime I came to Sardinia on holiday; I met Savin Couëlle because he was building a house for my parents. I was in the first year of

architecture and he was already lecturing. Then I spent a long time in Paris, where I completed my training.

G.B.: Do you maintain that architectural theories are useless to build houses in Sardinia?

Béthoux: Yes. What we are doing here is very different from major architectural objects. We are building houses for holidays, where you come to rest and relax. This has got little to do with architecture for large areas. I can spend my holidays in a tent, it doesn't matter; a holiday home is not an object that necessarily has to remain. "Architecture" is public money spent for an important building that has to remain for centuries. Like the Louvre, restored by a Chinese-American artist: I. Pei. Who knows how long it will last. What we are doing here, on the other hand, does not have this fate. Perhaps one day they will raze everything to the ground and build something else. Recently I have had clients who come to their house in low season or plan to use it more when they have retired. This gives greater involvement to the design and makes it less spectacular. I have seen, especially in Porto Rotondo, houses that look like film sets more than anything else... they also look out of place. They are hardly related to anything, they are just images flung there from pure imagination. They probably have a very ephemeral life because the imagination is a little like memory: it's something that today is fine and tomorrow no longer gives satisfaction: I have to throw it away and begin again.

G.B.: The holiday home as a home for dreams and freedom. And so also of freedom of expression?

Béthoux: I have designed a house that is twice as large as my standard. The owners did not understand a thing and they had it painted with frescoes in the style of a Venetian villa, like the house in the country they already have. Fabrics, false antiques, period paintings which are fine in a convent and not in a house by the sea... They have created a little part of their big house on the mainland. In my opinion, they haven't understood a thing. Not even about holidays: how can I come to Sardinia and see the same things that I have in my usual home? What have I come here for? I've missed out on half the purpose of the journey... The house has to be different, simple. It has to make you think of different universes. I don't have a style: it's the approach that is important. Of course, the ingredients are related to this land, to the image that the first architects of the Costa Smeralda gave to this place. Nothing existed here, they had to invent a local style, because the houses that existed here before, at least in this part of Sardinia, were very elementary: shepherds' houses or of small peasants,

like houses drawn by children, with a door in the middle and windows, and the chimney. In the meantime, however, this house does have ingredients, like the pantiles and stones, which are elements that can be found in houses all over the Mediterranean. And so they thought of importing everything that can be found in the Mediterranean. One sought inspiration in Tunisian houses or in the Greek islands, another built Provençal or Spanish houses. In the end a very specific style was born, which links up to the elements of this land: granite, the use of large openings we find nowhere else, like these sliding partitions, which make indoors and outdoors communicating.

G.B.: In your houses there are effects of vaults and arches intersecting. A fascinating architectural effect. Where does it come from?

Béthoux: I am a great admirer of spontaneous architecture, buildings made without architects, by very skilful master builders. I try to restore, if I can, especially on small budgets which do not allow important architectural solutions, an impression of something built that recalls the stability and method of always. These are houses of stone as in Europe. The house that offers shelter, almost primitive. But, on the contrary of the traditional homes which are too closed in on themselves, I try to open them with a lot of windows to let the light in. You have to build houses that are very flexible for their running and which can be modified. And so openings with sliding frames that move well and that open and close easily. You have to be limited in the "effects". Then houses become truer and more fluid. And then I try to avoid fashions. When I began working here, people wanted rustic houses, with poor materials. Now the fashion of aged materials is coming back into fashion. Like jeans, which from blue became faded, leather has to be worn... the same thing goes for houses. We use wood given a patina of age: if it is used well it works and gives the charm of old things.

G.B.: Architects have a great responsibility in Sardinia. Houses are now changing hands and this is a fact, as are the different requirements of the new owners. The first architects set a fashion for their clients. What is your relationship with your clients?

Béthoux: There is always an exchange between the client and the architect, there is mutual enrichment. Here, in relation to other places by the sea, much greater attention is paid to the garden, because it is a term of comparison. I try to follow the garden as well and the interior decoration, in order not to create completely different elements. In all, in twenty years I have not built very many houses, I am a craftsman and so I cannot develop a lot of work. Here you have to follow the work on site very carefully, especially for certain detail of work.

G.B.: Which materials do you like best?

Béthoux: We always use the same ingredients, at least we have a strong characteristic of relationship with nature and tradition. The desire to go back to the roots and the earth is increasingly strong. Sardinia is a country that plummeted from the Middle Ages to the twentieth century... Traditions are very strong. Even the harsh character of the people is part of what must be felt in the houses. I adopt solutions that seem poor and simple but which are not really so. I use craft materials and so they are more expensive than luxury materials. And as an image they are very beautiful, they have the sensitivity of what is completely handmade. But in Sardinia, it is already an adventure to build a house, because you never know whether the building permission is going to arrive, if the builders will keep to schedule, if the old wooden furnace that fires the tiles will break down. You have to deserve it. Thanks to certain architects, there are now qualified personnel who are unbeatable at certain things: on plasters, on giving shapes to arches, on laying ceramics. You have to work with the eye. Satisfy the eye and not the line.

G.B.: Your villas, even the most recent ones, are never too glaring in their appearance. What is your secret?

Béthoux: Plaster here is made of lime, there is no cement in it. It dissolves and fades in time, with the sun, the wind and the changes in temperature. It varies and takes on this variety of shades of colour which are its beauty. Of course, there is also the commercial factor, you have to use the materials that are available. And so you can use modern plaster and give it a patina to look old... You have to look for solutions like this. The same goes for wood, when stripped, a new element in the middle of old things goes very well together. They are porous materials and they make you want to touch them. By putting all these elements together you can do something right. You have to know how to use the tools, without making a "mock" old house. I put some elements that have a story in my houses, but the house has to function is a modern way, "breathe well" and be bright. But in the meantime, it reminds me of volumes I have already known, that are the volumes of memory and I try to avoid letting myself go to pure imagination, that only seems proper.

G.B.: Your architecture shows traces of a rationalist training. I feel that your curves are not the curves of the houses by Jacques Couëlle.

Béthoux: His houses have beautiful angles but inside you feel a bit oppressed. I find certain passages boring. Imagination is such a wonderful thing but I don't want a person to feel a stranger in his own home, or to move around as if he were in a museum. There are people with great insight who live very well in Couëlle's houses just as architects at times impose houses in which they themselves would not live.

G.B.: In Sardinia some villages have gone into complete decline in just a few years. Here, in San Pantaleo, I see a remarkably intact environment.

Béthoux: I have tried to set an example with a renovation using "pietra pinta" in the village square. The "pietra pinta" is a stone with the typical Gallura surfacing. Wide surfacing, astride the interstices. You can see the stone with these red junctions. The mason I worked with had already worked with Jacques Couëlle in the 1970s when he built his first house on Monte Mannu.

1965: Luigi Vietti with the Prince Karim Aga Khan.
"This photograph describes the real atmosphere of the beginnings of the first Costa Smeralda"
says the architect Jean-Paul De Marchi, who was an eye-witness.
"In addition to Luigi Vietti, there were only four architects on the project: Michele Busiri Vici, Antonio Simon Mossa, Jacques Couëlle and Raimond Martin".
Historic photos by: Nello Di Salvo (by courtesy of Laura, for no less than thirty years secretary of the "maestro" and of her husband Vanni Fiori).

Luigi Vietti

AN ARCHITECT OF NATURE. Luigi Vietti began his career in 1928 and worked continuously until his death in March 1998. He not only designed buildings but also worked on town planning, including the schemes for Cortina d'Ampezzo and Portofino as well as that for the Costa Smeralda in Sardinia. On the request of the Aga Khan in 1962, he then worked for many years with a group of architects building Porto Cervo and, amongst the countless summer homes of the international jet set to be recalled in particular is the highly exclusive Hotel Pitrizza in Liscia di Vacca, one of the most elegant in the world and where he poetically applied his principles of fusion between what construction and nature. "The roofs were all to be in the midst of greenery, without being seen from the sea, the buildings are low, made of local stone, the very famous swimming pool overflows becoming one with the sea...". Of all his works, Vietti was always fondest of the last one, but if he really had to choose, he would name his home on the Costa Smeralda, "La Cerva", a villa built on one of the points that encloses the bay of Porto Cervo, as one of his most successful designs. It is made up of low volumes which follow the unevenness of the land and penetrate or withdraw from the surrounding nature with the climbing plants and shrubs of the Mediterranean vegetation forming an integral part of the villa in a luxuriant embrace. This embrace that appears casual was expertly designed by Vietti, in search of an effect which is never theatrical but "pure", simple and rational. The materials used are those offered locally: rocks, monolithic granite for the pillars, knotty juniper beams for the ceilings. Nature enters into the construction and becomes architecture in the corridor separating the rooms with a ceiling made of a bower, a live "heartbeat" inside the house.

*Villa "La Cerva" cannot be seen
from the land or from the sea. The materials used both inside
and outside evoke the surrounding nature, such as stones and wood.
The distribution of the rooms is extremely linear: a wide open space is
devoted to the sitting-room, divided into different areas
emphasized by the effect of the visible roof.*

On the left the exterior of the villa with monolithic granite pillars.
On the right Vietti's first floor study with one of his many collections of model
antique sailing-ships. _Below_ the corridor connecting the bedrooms.
On the facing page the famous corridor-gallery
with its ceiling formed by a bower. The synthesis of the poetics of Vietti:
fusion and camouflage between human work and nature.

The large sitting-room is divided
into different corners. Here
we can see the conversation corner
with the sofas facing the panorama
taking in the whole of the bay.
The ceiling here is sloping to
emphasize and frame this corner.
The architecture also
converges towards the large
picture windows
with their enchanting view.
A space has been left behind the
sofa to be used as a passage and
a lowered step is used as a
bench filled with cushions.
Along the wall, masonry shelves
contain books and displays
models of ancient galleons, one of
Vietti's countless collections.

*On the facing page, above the patio with the outside dining-area.
Note how the villa has been built according to the principle of maximum integration
with the surrounding environment and the materials are the same here as inside.
On the facing page, below the bedroom furnished with a combination of
Sardinian antiques and design furniture made by local craftsmen.
Above, in perfect harmony, stone and ceramic busts,
white plaster and open beams, polished terracotta
tiles and wrought iron.*

Vanni Fiori

TECHNOLOGY AND TRADITION. This would appear a contradiction in terms, but Fiori's greatest merit is that of meeting the needs of villa "renovation" in the most delightful spots of the Costa Smeralda, without betraying their spirit, skilfully combining the most advanced technologies with a culture of the territory which he possesses, not only thanks to technical studies and personal research but also because he is the only Sardinian designer working here. Everything echoes his inspiration, from the traditions of Sardinian crafts, which he has always known, to his long experience as a surveyor which makes him unequalled in his familiarity and "photographic" appreciation of areas, measurements, differences in levels and to the long periods he spent with Luigi Vietti. Fiori was always chosen by Vietti to supervise the execution of his designs and, both in his studio or outside as a partner, the pupil became familiar from a very early age with the master's themes. In this part of the book, from the countless projects of Fiori we have chosen the emblematic restoration of a house built in Porto Cervo Marina in the 1980s. Standing in one of the most exclusive spots, very close to the harbour and where the greenery is lush and abundant, it faces south-west and enjoys a magnificent view. The designer's transformations have been essential and the technological solutions are well camouflaged. The entrance which penalized the relaxation area and the swimming pool has been revolutionized. Due to legislative reasons, the "open" perimeter and disposition of the accomodation have been maintained whilst Fiori's ability lies in hidden volumes and in the agreeable outdoor areas, with the barbecue-dining area standing out here. Thanks to sophisticated lighting, in the evening the villa is mirrored in its blue swimming pool and plays at effects of lights and shadows with the enchanting view of the surrounding garden, again designed by Fiori's firm and landscaped by Sgaravatti Mediterranea.

A seductive corner that shows
the designer's exquisite sensitivity for materials.
Fiori, like his master Vietti, appreciates local materials and has the
special grace of inserting the building into its landscape. In this case too,
he has preserved the charm of the place, enlarging the open-air
areas and enhancing the swimming pool area.

Proud of his Sardinian origins,
Fiori restores the traditional
instruments of Sardinian living
to high,level architecture.
He is a fervent supporter
of barbecues and in general
roasting on open fires.
This is the innovative part
of his project, a porch
next to the indoor dining room,
with a real outdoor dining area.
The solarium on the roof
of the lounge
and the swimming pool
are reached from here.

*The lounge is characterized
by the large picture windows looking
on to the swimming pool area with
lights set into the ceiling and the
interior decoration including some
fine antique pieces from Bologna,
where the owners also come from.*

*On this page the details emphasizing
the skilful use of local materials. The dry walls are built of Gallura field stones,
the porch ceiling is made of canes, the dining table is made of yellow granite, the triangular tiles
in the bathroom have been handmade to design by Petra Sarda of San Pantaleo.*

*On the facing page, above the entrance porch with a "Vietti-style" granite pillar.
Below the bedroom with a Banci four-poster bed.*

Jacques Couëlle

INHABITABLE SCULPTURE. An architect who is hard to classify, except as a follower of architecture-sculpture. In this house he designed, the sense of sculpture tends to cover up that of pure rationality. The first attempts at sculpture-architecture were made by the artistic avant-garde of the first decade of the century and, in the majority of cases, sculptors were the ones to take the first step, led by Malevich and then architects such as Van Doesburg and Gerrit Rietveld. But the first architectures-sculptures were monolithic dispositions of volumes without a real solution for inner space and true utopias. Besides, architecture, by its very own definition, has to be "built" and inhabited and it can indeed be said that architects need clients to express their designs. The economic recession of the 1930s and then the war set aside avant-garde research especially as far as homes were concerned. In the second half of the 1950s, the debate was resumed both by architects and sculptors, resulting in the flourishing evolution of the next decade, especially in highly industrialized countries, where the way was paved by the development of technology and economic growth. It was in this context which favoured a spirit of adventure, utopian research and innovation that architecture-sculpture found its forms. It was in the early 1960s that Szekeli and Couëlle made sculptures with a composite disposition of volumes that could be inhabited. This blend of architecture and sculpture is rarely taken seriously in official histories of architecture. The first study which classified it as one of the five components of organic architecture was by Bruno Zevi who wrote: "Sculpted architecture is conceived as a rock full of holes and which can be inhabited like troglodytes' caves", but for others, it is a scenario lacking in consistency.

In the sculpture-house of Monte Mannu in Sardinia,
Couëlle built the most famous sculpture-home for himself.
Facing pages and the following pages, playing with primitive volumes, Couëlle
achieves a perfect symbiosis between the house and the surrounding nature.
Multi-coloured ceramic tiles form the "skin" of this building with
curved lines shaped in cement and applied on metal structures.

However, Couëlle's way of building always refers to man and the remarkable test he put his client to is perfect evidence of this. His inhabitable structures, as he himself defined them, began with five prototypes of dwellings built in Castellaras, near Cannes, for a village with more than fifty units, a home for himself in Sardinia on Monte Mannu (the one presented in these pages), then the project of a house for several families in Frankfurt. Couëlle called his method for designing the lay-out of the rooms "Tristan's Test". "In situ", the architect had the actual plan with the main rooms traced out and then sprinkled with flour or sand. Then he would invite the future occupants of the house to mime their routes and the actions they carry out in each room. Their traces are then photographed and were used by the architect to better identify the area for each individual function. The result of this attention to the physiological as well as emotional needs of individuals is clearly not a standard apartment but, on the contrary, a shell modelled around the needs and desires of each individual client. Moreover, his sculpture-homes are inspired by the poetics of body language, gestural expressiveness which is amplified in curved shapes and never at right angles.

Above two details: the swimming pool carved out of the rock and the staircase with its sensual juniper wood balcony. On the facing page, the niche in the wall bears the prints of Couëlle's hands. On the following pages other details: the polychromatic facing of the windows experienced as "eyes" looking at the landscape, so that the experience is not only visual but also emotional and tactile.

Savin Couëlle

INTEGRAL COMMUNION WITH THE ISLAND. This is the philosophy underlying all the homes of this very famous architect whose name is strongly linked to Sardinia and in particular to the Costa Smeralda. Born in Aix-en-Provence in 1929, after his degree in architecture, he worked as assistant set designer with the very famous George Wakhevitch and Alexandre Trauner and then he designed the sets for major film productions such as "The King of Kings", "El Cid" and "The Fall of the Roman Empire". At the beginning of the 1960s, he discovered Sardinia in the wake of his father Jacques who wanted his collaboration on the ambitious project the Prince Aga Khan had assigned to him: to design the residential complex of the Costa Smeralda. Savin immediately gave in to the fascination of this uncontaminated nature with centuries-old traditions and where there were more buildings inland than on the coast. The huge granite rocks shaped by the wind become objects of cult to be protected and lead him to elaborate an architectonic philosophy with a naturalistic hallmark that he is never to give up. The house we have chosen belongs to a small complex standing on the inaccessible hill dominating Porto Cervo, about two kilometres from the sea and at 250 metres above sea level. The houses were built in absolute total respect of nature and indeed the rock formations with their bizarre profiles, modelled over the centuries by the wind and water, have taken on leading roles, majestically becoming part of the interior decoration. The mimesis with nature is complete, both in the shape which is in harmony with the terrain and in the materials and soft shades of the plaster. "La tana del cervo" ("The deer's lair") is an appropriate name for this complex which has resisted over the years appearing always new and, naturally, always ancient, just like a Tibetan monastery.

*The complex of dwellings is adapted to the steep rocky wall
in the shapes and colours of the materials. The strangely-shaped rocks, protected by
the Italian Fine Arts Trust, have influenced the whole project. Incorporated into the
structure, they become a supporting element and decoration at the same time.
Homes that seem to have come into being spontaneously, refuge-dwellings
where time appears to have been cancelled.*

*On this page the construction details which as well as following
the unevenness of the ground use local materials such as stone, the plaster obtained
from the earth and grinding tiles salvaged from the "stazzu", the local shepherds' shelter.
On the facing page rock as the protagonist of a corner in the lounge.*

On these pages
all the constructive skill of Savin Couëlle
who has made the rock formations
the leit-motiv of his designs.
Years of patience
were required to complete it,
precisely because of the difficulties
of the location.
The reward is the superb insertion
into the natural context,
the timeless taste of these dwellings:
on a human and environmental scale.

*Below the bedroom is given movement by the structure
of the wall which is moulded on the very rock which forms part of the lounge ceiling.
On the facing page the bathroom, renovated together with the kitchen by the
architect Gérard Béthoux at a later date. Respecting the philosophy of
the general outlay, he has created sinuous lines emphasized
by the ceramic facing.*

Ferdinando Fagnola

A VILLA BORN OUT OF THE EARTH. This Turin-born architect has left his mark on the Costa Smeralda with this very remarkable villa, located near Portisco and built in the early 1980s. The house has an uninhibited plan which is completely open and articulated in such a way as to ensure a continuous relationship with the outside. Built of cement and wood, half below ground level so that it cannot be seen, this villa seems to emerge from the earth with its slender drilled metal sheeting weathercock. Only natural materials have been used in this building, with its load-bearing cement walls and open iron I-beams. The architect has interpreted mimesis with nature in the general organisation of the accomodation. The grass-covered roof and the low and oblique volumes evoke the tents of nomads squatting in front of the sea and rising out of a pocket in the land. The architect has achieved this difficult result by decomposing the building into volumes articulated around a patio and the "destructuring" of the perspectives. The materials are left free to live out their "decadence" according to the natural processes of oxidation and ageing. The external parts in wood are made of untreated essence of iroko. Some parts are made of "corten steel", a material which reddens as it ages. Cement, widely used and interpreted as artificial rock has been "bushhammered" on the surface to make it look more like the local stone. The interior walls have been given a very fine whitewash glaze, ranging in shade from yellow to red, leaving the weft of the caissons visible. The lounge where the cement has been left natural, although very large and below ground level, has excellent natural lighting thanks to the frontal windows looking on to the patio and the rift between the two pitches of the roof which forms a strip of zenithal light on the floor, following the movement of the sun like a sundial. The plants, skilfully trained by the architect Paolo Pejrone, invade and confuse the volumes, clothe the sloping roofs, soften sharp edges and mark a new and long-standing relationship between the house and time.

On the facing page, above the house squatting on the land is very well camouflaged in the landscape thanks to the roofs sown with grass and the oblique volumes built of materials that easily blend into the presence of the surrounding nature. Below the indoor passage with the large windows that look on to the garden. This patio separates the day area from the night area.

*Another view of the patio
sheltered from the wind
and surrounded by jasmine.
This is the heart of the house
that lets it breathe and get direct light.
Of interest is the surrounding nature
"tamed" by landscape architect
Paolo Pejrone near the patio
with butterbush and jasmine
for Mediterranean-scented relaxation.
The flooring and furniture
are made of teak.*

Anticipating current architectural trends by 20 years,
from a structural point of view the villa does not have pillars
but only load bearing walls. There is a lot of "bushhammered" cement
to make its surface look more like the local granite,
a lot of "corten steel" which reddens as it rusts like the mould on rock,
untreated "iroko wood" which takes on the silver hue
of the nearby cliffs as it dries in the sun. <u>On this page above</u>
the dining room. The walls are made of bushhammered cement.
The wooden and industrial iron table has a revolving tray.
The Indonesian totem in the corner is part
of the owner's collection of primitive art. <u>On the facing page</u>
a view of the lounge, with mat flooring and rope
replacing the skirting board.

The lounge, surprisingly bright, has its ceiling divided into
two large cement pitches, separated by a very long continuous glass embrasure,
allowing the sun to enter zenithally, drawing its movement on the floor,
which thus automatically becomes a giant sundial.
<u>*Above*</u>*, the lounge where the furniture and finishes have been*
customized to set off to the best the owners' collection of primitive art.
<u>*On the facing page*</u>*,* <u>*above*</u>*, the other seaward view from the patio.*
<u>*Below*</u> *the master bedroom. Here the cement of the walls has been*
"sponged" with a marked touch of colour.

Paul-Auguste Gilliot

ENVIRONMENTALIST AND ECOLOGIST. The French, or rather "mountain" architect as he defines himself, built this small 60 square metre house for himself in the 1970s. Instead of choosing the Costa Smeralda and although he was part of the team of international fame that the Aga Khan summoned around 1968, he preferred a secluded place high up near San Pantaleo. The house, perched on a promontory with Porto Cervo and Porto Rotondo a sheer drop below, ostentatiously ignores the sea at its feet offering its inhabitants a view of bare almost Dolomite-like mountains. In fact, the small house in San Pantaleo really seems to belong to the environment it stands in and has the "lived in" appearance of a renovated cottage rather than of a house built from scratch. Paul-Auguste Gilliot, today Superintendent for Fine Arts for the whole of south-western France, who came with Jacques Couëlle, also wanted to be ecological in his choice of the design, a small "mock" old house. Built in ups and downs to match the uneven lie of the land, although in practical terms consisting of a simple rectangular volume, movement is given by stone steps and wooden ladders, like the ones found in haylofts, to move from one room to another. In a word, this is a minimal but very warm house, where great attention has been paid to every detail. Space is not that important, says Gilliot, especially for someone like me who is used to living in small areas. The important thing is to design each single niche or "crevice" and keep things tidy, just like on a boat. The space is conceived for everything to be interlocking, with the entrance also doubling as a cosy dining-room, the kitchen is separated from the dining area by shelves with a mezzanine overlooking it. The lounge has a large fireplace surrounded by sofas made of masonry. There are also two bedrooms, each with its own bathroom.

The entrance opens directly on to the dining area and, going up a few granite steps, on to the lounge with its big fireplace.
On the following pages the rectangular volume of the house which fully respects the idea of a cottage renovated according to the lie of the land and in sixty square metres successfully comprises a kitchen, dining room, lounge and two bedrooms with their own bathrooms.

The illusion of being in a real cottage that has been readapted
is the effect that the mountain-loving French architect has succeeded in achieving
in his mini house in San Pantaleo. He has been guided by his instinct for the materials
to use and his affectionate study of Sardinian rural dwellings, the famous
"stazzus". The only whimsical concession of modern sensitivity
are the windows which are not only of different sizes
but are genuine "pictures", offering deliberately
framed portions of landscape.

On the left, a detail of the
bookcase in the lounge.
A genuine love for Sardinia,
discovered at the end of the 1960s
with his friend Jacques Couëlle,
underlies the whole design, both of the
exterior and in the materials.
Below, hidden amongst the
shelves and the small collections
of animals, there is a tiny window,
almost a peep-hole, looking on to
the greenery. _On the right_, a view
of the kitchen, separated from the
dining-room by open shelving.
Every object is in its place and has
been carefully chosen from the
extremely rich variety of
traditional Sardinian crafts.

Gianni Gamondi

A DESIGNER OF DREAMS. Graduating in Milan the same year as Renzo Piano, this rationalist has always devoted himself to tourism for the élite. Moreover, he also created Porto Rotondo, a real village conceived around an open square looking on to the sea and encircled by arcades. His villas are amongst the most beautiful and "customized" on the Costa Smeralda: he is an architect who knows how to interpret the personality of the villa's inhabitant, whether it is a VIP from the world of fashion, such as the designer Krizia whose home opens this chapter, a magnate or a politician. He skilfully orchestrates volumes on a human scale and builds stone bungalows with a semi-embedded ground floor, grass-covered roofs and dry stone external walls. Whether built on the site of a previous cottage and surrounded by a plot of land with a surface area of seventy thousand square metres like the villa of a well known Milanese entrepreneur which is his refuge and manor, almost resembling a turreted hamlet of ancient memory, or a design based on the differentiation of volumes highlighting the different parts making up the villa, the result is always a building with an effect that is anything but static. It is difficult to choose from his beautiful homes: here we have chosen four which interpret Gamondi's architecture as well as the needs of his clients. Moreover, with his shy character, he defines himself not as a genius but as a serious professional person. "I don't have the vocation to leave my architectural mark at all costs. Let's leave that difficult job to the geniuses and poets like Wright. I consider myself a normal professional person who mediates between architecture and nature, knowing and accepting that of the two the latter wins".

The villa belonging to the fashion designer Krizia
is one of the most successful interpretations of the Gamondi style.
Villa and nature are blended in perfect symbiosis. The rooms, closed or open, follow
the level of the land like the spontaneous aggregation of a geometric body or a cell
that replicates itself. The materials used are Sardinian, natural rough-shaped
or dressed natural granite and wood.

The very large lounge with big picture windows is divided into several areas.
<u>On the previous page</u> the right corner of the fireplace which opens on to the entrance.
Iroko wood and granite have been used for the floors, both indoors and
outdoors, in different proportions and finishes.

The indoor and outdoor
spaces are articulated
with the same simplicity,
almost a harmonic
correspondence
and a reflecting mirror.
On the veranda, the large table
at the focal point
of the area was made to
measure from iroko wood.
Its base has four granite legs.
The solid chairs are
made of teak. _Below left_
a detail of the master bedroom.
Near the door, lacquered blue
like all those in the house,
there is a picture with a
panorama by Randol Morgan
and an antique Thonet chair.
Below right the reverse angle
shot of the bedroom with
a view of the veranda.
Above the bed there is
a semi-circular picture
by Pardi.

GIANNI GAMONDI

Like a fortified village overlooking the bay

This large villa stands at the tip of the promontory of Punta Lada, near Porto Rotondo. It is hard to recognize the harsh and wild sea of Sardinia here, where nature seems calmer and more bucolic, less tormented by the winds. The sound of the sea is also muffled by the time it reaches the villa across the huge garden. Gianni Gamondi built the villa on a pre-existing rural dwelling and kept the differences of the original volumes linked by a roof which, articulated at different heights, creates the effect of an old village.

A Milanese entrepreneur has made this his exclusive refuge; here the dreams of the client have encountered the interpreter-architect who has given form to the owner's wishes and expressed the mark of local nature in intelligent harmony.

Here the colours seem to want to imitate those of the light which at dawn gives rhythm to each volume: from pink to ochre. The roofs are covered with salvaged tiles in order not to clash with the choice of shades mellowed by the sea air into "colour of time" hues.

The garden, created together with the building, as is Gamondi's habit, by Sgaravatti Mediterranea, is dotted with the typical plants of a maritime climate, including olive-trees and juniper.

The varying dispositions of volumes making up the body of the villa correspond to a ground floor with, as is usual, a dining room, lounge and study; a first floor with six suites, two of which are master suites each with its own study, walk-in wardrobe, bathroom and veranda. At the lowest level, underground because the house follows the slope of the land, is the swimming pool with a hydro-massage bath and sauna, the kitchen, laundry, staff quarters and a store-room.

*Built on a pre-existing rural house,
the villa enjoys an enviable position on the promontory of Punta Lada.
Built for a Milanese entrepreneur with its well orchestrated volumes, it recalls
a medieval turreted village. The way it has been carefully inserted into
the landscape and the excellent design of the garden make it a
very fine and unique gem.*

On this page, above
the porch with bushhammered pink granite columns.
The table top is made by Unopiù of concrete with iron legs, like the chairs.
Below the circular drive at the entrance with a windrose mosaic made
of river pebbles and granite. *On the facing page* the magnificent lounge
reflects the owner's taste for antiques with furniture from the studio of Bartolozzi
and Maioli, Florence. *Above* the conversation area furnished with sofas by
Pozzoli with Sergio Rossi upholstery. The low Chinese table is by Consolo.
Below the dining-room with a 19th century extendible
table and trompe-l'oeil which repeats the
view enjoyed on the opposite side,
photo on the following page.

This large pool area has been built in the basement of the villa. The open space comprises a swimming pool, in the background an octagonal bath with hydro-massage and, separated by the mirror-covered wall, the sauna. The outdoor-indoor effect is emphasized by the refined trellising by the Carugati joinery which covers the walls and by the trompe-l'oeils by Giordana and Prato which brighten the lounge corner with its carefully chosen furnishing, as in all the other rooms, by "La Mariposa" of Puntaldia. Fabrics by Rossi of Rovezzano, furniture by Gasparucci and Cugini Lanzani and antique furniture by Stoppino.

A refuge between the sea and the garden

This villa camouflaged by greenery only thirty metres from the sea was built in the early 1970s. Originating as a wager to design something of absolute mimesis in an enchanting and uncontaminated place, Punta Volpe, a promontory that lies at the extreme eastern tip of the area of Porto Rotondo, linked to

the dry land by the narrow isthmus that separates Liscia Segata from Cala su Pinnone. Here the plots of land are large, about six thousand square metres. The house is perfectly camouflaged in the surrounding environment as it has been built snugly against a small hill, with its grass blending in with the roof of the house. The roof is in fact covered by grass to respect the aim of Gamondi and his partner at that time Antonioli, but in tacit agreement with all the major architects working in that part of Sardinia: the mimesis between architecture and nature.

Built snugly against a hill just a few metres from the sea, this villa is the manifesto of Gamondi's style. The total mimesis between the building and the landscape. The walls are dry-stone, the whole volume is below ground level and the roof is covered with grass.

The effect of non-volume from the outside
is transformed indoors into a cosy atmosphere full of corners
that frame the view through the large windows opening
on to the greenery. <u>Below</u> relaxation with a sea view
from two hammocks.

The spectacular intervention
of the wooden creations by
Ascanio Palchetti,
a craftsman in interior
decoration with a late
vocation, gives a unique
character to some parts
of the lounge.
Born near Genoa,
a ski instructor, sports manager,
water-skiing instructor,
involved in the production
of go-carts with the
Donà Delle Rose Counts
in the 1960s, Palchetti
has left his "mark" on many
exclusive clubs and villas
on the Costa Smeralda.
Opposite his own house, in front
of the church built by Ceroli,
he designed a fountain for
animals, worthy of a poet.

*On this page, above a view of the villa, with its
dry walls built of field granite blending into the landscape.
Below durmast sofas, coffee-tables and rocking-chairs have been placed looking on to
the sea, in the shade of the cane roof, for a siesta with a sea view.
The pinewood porch structure is painted green.*

*On the facing page the master bedroom.
It occupies a large area on two levels, with the bedroom part,
a small lounge and the bathroom. The specially designed furniture is made
of pinewood as are the beams. The woollen rugs are hand-woven in the Sardinian
craft tradition, as are the filet bedspread and the late nineteenth-century pillows.*

In Sardinia as in the Bahamas...

In this villa, Gamondi has taken the opportunity to restore one of his own houses built twenty years previously and give a new look to the ideal of construction which for years he has pursued on this part of the coast which he dearly loves and knows. After his association with the fashion designer Krizia, the architect created on Barbuda the very exclusive club "K" which bears the indelible mark of his style: simplicity, rigour, "lightness" but also precision and the culture of local materials.

leitmotiv, but which also blends very easily with the purest Mediterranean style. The slabs of the roof used as a garden are new, sown with grass, as is the central patio with the day and night areas built around it and the veranda built entirely of wood is also new, as are the sliding doors and windows which occupy a whole wall. The stone facing and the arcades of the perimeter, marking the gradual passage between nature and construction, have remained as they were.

We can recognize in this villa a desire for radiant white, in the panelled door and window frames and in the ceiling of the porch which recalls the colonial

The surrounding nature, masterfully worked into a garden with the scents of the Mediterranean vegetation are the work of Gamondi and Sgaravatti Mediterranea.

On the previous page
the large lounge separated from
the porch by a large window.
These "squared" window frames
and the use of white underlining the
window panes and porches recalls
certain leitmotivs of the architecture
of the Southern states of the USA,
where the owner of the villa comes
from. This atmosphere can also be felt
in the choice of the furniture. The
irregularly shaped swimming pool,
looking on to the sea, seems to reflect
the villa's "undulated" façade
and has a granite edge.

The indoor furniture is informal and pleasant,
mixing wicker pieces with nineteenth century furniture and lamps;
the French woollen carpet is an antique. <u>On the facing page</u>, <u>above</u> the kitchen
and the table with a Carrara marble top. The custom-designed furniture was made
of pearl white painted wood by the Sala joinery in Brianza. The walls
have an encaustic finish. The veranda has an old kitchen table and
trellis-covered walls. <u>On the facing page</u>, <u>below</u> the guest room. The bed is
made from two old English divans. The walls have striped wallpaper.
The exuberance of the flower-patterned fabric, cleverly blended
in a mock casual style recalls the best of the "homely"
style of Anglo-Saxon houses.

Gérard Béthoux

THE TRIUMPH OF MEDITERRANEAN TRADITION.
From the first generation of architects we can go on to the second,
with a return to the rustic dwellings and villas already built in the most
enchanting spots of the Costa Smeralda for their adaptation to other
clients with different requirements. Imagination and attention to even
the smallest detail; a solid knowledge of the trade and techniques; an
intelligent use of materials, especially wood and granite. When the
touch of Sardinian crafts is not enough, one can confidently look
outside the island. Few flowers are planted outside but there is a lot of
mediterranean maquis. If the spot is too flat, then rocky fill-ins are
invented to give movement to the swimming pool... and this could
even be its natural state: but it has in fact been re-created and
everything is the result of accurate research. "The first thing that should
be taken into account when designing a house is how to position it
best to the cardinal points as well as achieving the most attractive
view", says architect Béthoux. The skill lies in creating rooms both
outdoors and indoors in perfect harmony, taking advantage of the
staggered levels, recreating movements of land which justify the
different levels. According to the design, which always follows the rule
of using techniques and materials that are as traditional as possible, the
swimming pool and the garden become part of a game of
counterpoint, in symbiosis with the building, the unicum between two
distinct projects called renovation, which gives a meaningful conclusion
to the work.

This villa in Piccolo Romazzino was built in co-operation with
the architect Careddu. The interior decoration is by Eva Beckwith.
The real challenge was to include in the construction a pre-existent
unrefined structure, designed by the architect Savin Couëlle.
Traditional Mediterranean materials have been used: for the exterior,
a lot of granite, light-coloured or pink-tinged plasters, a double
layer of old tiles for the roofing.

The terrace outside the lounge which looks on to the pool is a few metres above the level of the water and is covered by canes, given an even more rustic effect by the raffia strand fringe. The terracotta floor is the same as in the lounge. The wicker armchairs and sofas come from the Wicker Work collection; thick-striped fabric by Pierre Frey covers the upholstery.

*In the details <u>below left</u>
a view from the very picturesque
pool looking towards the veranda.
<u>In the centre</u> the veranda next
to the kitchen with the barbecue.
This outdoor dining area
is partly sheltered by a cane roof
and by large parasols.
<u>On the left</u> a view of the entrance.
The light comes from the pool
which "comes into the house"
through a window
in the wall.*

<u>On this page</u>, <u>above left</u>
the view of the master bedroom
with a wicker dormeuse in the centre
of the large picture window
which looks on to the garden
and which can be seen <u>in close up on the facing page</u>.
<u>Above right</u> a detail of the den
which has a vaulted ceiling and opens on to the rockery
and plants outdoors, through an arched window.
The base of the sofas is made of stone,
the furniture has been custom designed and made
of pickled elm. <u>Below left</u> the fireplace with
a bushhammered granite surround with
two modern Chinese vases as embellishments.

*On this page the area linking the dining room
and the lounge which can be seen on the facing page. Thanks to the
effect of the arches, the masonry, with an interesting effect of arrangement of volumes,
not only successfully plays the function of joining the rooms - the staircase
leading to the bedrooms also opens on to this area - but becomes
the real focus of the day area.*

Designed to make the landscape live

This complete renovation in a small area surrounded by other buildings is in Porto Rafael, a holiday complex south of Palau. Here too there are the characteristic rock formations and the sea view is enriched by the outlines of the archipelago of La Maddalena with the isle of Santo Stefano in the foreground. A delightful spot that Gérard Béthoux has succeeded in bringing into the house, like wonderful pictures to be admired, thanks to his arrangement of windows and openings. The house is built on two levels, with a barbecue and outdoor lounge on staggered levels. The outdoor details have a clear Mediterranean flavour dominated by the pink-tinged harmony of the plaster echoing the warm hue of the terracotta outdoor flooring and the traditional tiles. A way of giving integrity to a dwelling and inserting the building into the surrounding nature. The colour scheme for the interior is based on white and blue and the custom-designed furniture is made of solid "cérusé" elm.

Great attention is paid to detail in the split level outdoor areas. <u>On the left</u> the outdoor lounge with craft-made iron armchairs supplied by the shop "Case e Cose l'Arredamento", Porto Rotondo. <u>On the right</u> the barbecue with the hand-made custom-designed table made of Spanish glazed terracotta, Andia.

The large photo
shows the different levels
of the house. In the foreground,
the lounge with a coffee-table.
Its large tray surface is made of
glazed terracotta. The upholstery
is French, the antique furniture
comes from the Milanese shop
"La Biscaglia". *In the small photo*
a view from the outdoor
lounge looking
indoors.

On the left the dining
area which is on a slightly different
level compared to the lounge, with
two arches joining them.
The floor is made of hand-glazed
Neapolitan terracotta.
On the right a detail of the wall in
which an "internal" window
has been opened, looking on to the
kitchen. Shelves and pharmacy vases
make a pleasant interruption
to the habitat.

On this page, <u>left</u>
the guest room has also been decorated in
the white and blue colour scheme predominating
throughout the house. The bedside lamps with a
fish-shaped terracotta base are craft-made.
<u>In the centre</u> the remarkable juniper
gate surrounded by an almost
"majestic" granite portal.

<u>In the photo below left</u>
a detail of the main bathroom which takes its
effect from the combination of white glazed terracotta
facings in different shapes. The mirrors are special designs
made by Caprotti. <u>On the facing page</u> the entirely
custom-designed kitchen. The furniture has white
doors with a blue trim and has been made
by the master Sardinian joinery of
the Savigni brothers.

An almost classic allmark

This villa in Cala di Volpe is more impressive, but the design again evokes the deliberately craft-like dimension of the house built like the fine homes of bygone times.

Built of stone with solid granite frames, without cement, the roof is supported by long and robust open beams.

The large lounge with its splendid six metre-long sliding window continues in the adjacent southern-facing porch, whilst on the other side it opens on to a patio laid out not only for barbecues and alfresco eating but also, thanks to the arch outlining the accomodation, as the architectural counterweight of a second façade. To sum up, a morphology which represents the two faces of Sardinia: the sea and the mountains.

*In this villa,
the large articulated pool
has been designed to fit
harmoniously into the surroundings
like a small artificial lake
with the water skimming
the bushhammered Sardinian granite edges,
emphasizing the pool's
irregular shape.*

129

*The outdoor areas have been designed by
Béthoux with great care and differentiated according to
their function. <u>Below</u> the relax area facing the pool has a
sophisticated cane roofing with a raffia trim.
<u>On the facing page</u> the table in the
outdoor dining area with barbecue is
made of decorated Valencia tiles.*

*<u>On the following page</u> the lounge
with the handmade "Ceramica Diemme" mother-of-pearl
glazed terracotta floor with different shaped tiles. The alder doors
were designed by the architect and made by the Cuneo-based
Valtorta joinery.*

Above two details of the kitchen with fittings in aged wood
in ochre and Sienna earth designed by the architect and made by the Cuneo-based
Valtorta joinery. Tiles by Andia of Valenza. *Below* the bedroom which opens on
to the bathroom *on the facing page*. Lozenge-shaped handmade
mother-of-pearl terracotta tiles by "Cotto Artigiano".

Two symmetrical porches to enjoy the summer

The concrete structure was more or less there, but the interior has been completely redesigned and a great deal has been done so that the volumes follow the lie of the land better. Gérard Béthoux and Sgaravatti Mediterranea made considerable modifications to the garden and most of all have tried to make the corner with the swimming

pool, on a bare and uninteresting stretch of land, more evocative. There were no rocks sculpted by the wind here but, with mechanical means, some boulders have been strategically positioned. The outdoors here too has been designed in order to create two alfresco areas, one for dining and with the barbecue, which is very cool in the summer, and the other for the lounge and relaxation near the pool. Juniper, a fragrant wood which cannot be attacked by insects, has been used for the two roofs, covered with canes, giving a rustic touch to the entrance. It has also been given a certain emphasis by a porch which was not included in the original design.

On the facing page the exterior of the villa with its harmonious accomodation thanks to the ingenious landfills and additional rocks. Below one of the two porches created on the two sides.

On this page, above left a detail of the juniper beam work which gives movement to the ceilings. *Right* the architectural element which gives the roof its finishing touch: the covering of tiles has been arranged in the traditional style, with the indented gutter, due to the fact that the channel tiles protrude more than the covering tiles. The result is a decoration that can be found in Provence and the whole of the Mediterranean basin. *Centre left* the fine porch by Giuseppe Frontello which enhances the entrance. The sanded durmast door was made by a craftsman in Arzachena. On either side, two large ornamental jars. *Right* a detail of the window on the façade with a very precisely shaped stone facing. This was specifically requested by the owner, who comes from Northern Europe. *Below left* one of the two porches. Here the table is made out of a single block of granite. *Alongside* a detail of the fresco decorating the wall-bar. It is by the Belgian artist Rudi Peipers and shows a map of the archipelago of La Maddalena. *Photo opposite* the shower in the large rock separating the relaxation area from the swimming pool.

The floor of the lounge is made of glazed terracotta tiles by Diemme, a long-standing company now belonging to Cesare Mori in Porto San Giorgio. The divans are built of masonry with side tables made of hand-cut granite.
In the original design there was a wall dividing the dining room from the lounge: this had to be kept.
The other end of the lounge was conceived for the fireplace to be used during the cooler periods of the year.
The furniture, lamps and objects are by Arcarosa.

*The master bedroom
looks on to the outside
through two large windows
and on to the golf course.
This is the largest bedroom
with a wrought iron
four-poster bed.
Fabrics by Maestro Raphael
and furnishings by Arcarosa.*

*The room is directly
inter-communicating with the
bathroom which is not large
but has a special touch
due to the window in the detail
shown on the right.
It is made with a small stainless steel
structure made by a smith in Olbia,
the central part of
which can be opened.*

The Gardens

THE MEDITERRANEAN GARDEN is the result of many years of study and research and can trace its origin back to the time when English landscape gardeners decided to seek inspiration in the gardens of Moorish origin in the south of Spain or imitate the large gardens of the Renaissance. The principles of the two schools of thought are diametrically opposed, but we shall see how, in the extraordinary effort to "invent" a style for gardens as well as for architecture on the Costa Smeralda, this union has been successful. What is the major difference between these two types of gardens? The Moorish garden is enclosed: it is a paradise in the midst of the desert and so it is protected by walls. Generally there is a fountain in the centre which cools the air during the hot summer months and sometimes the garden is divided into four parts separated by small canals symbolising the four rivers of life. The best examples are the gardens of the Alhambra in Granada and the Alcazar in Seville. The second style is that of the Italian Renaissance where the particularity lies in balance and proportion. Whilst the Moorish style is essential and designed to be used by people, the second is rich in collections of statues, balustrades, series of perspectives and was created to surprise and be admired. The examples presented here are all by very well-known architects such as Jacques Couëlle, who designed almost three hundred in his lifetime, and by Pietro Porcinai, the Tuscan landscape maestro, but also by the other architects we have met in these pages with the expert support first of Leone Sgaravatti, then of Giuseppe Carteri, of Sgaravatti Mediterranea. This synthesis gains in vigour from the extraordinary reality of the Costa Smeralda itself. "Everything began with the architects Michele and Giancarlo Busiri Vici with the gardens for the Hotel Romazzino and in the work with the great Gigi Vietti for the villa belonging to Alexandra of Kent at Piccolo Ramazzino", recalls Carteri.

On the right and on the following pages, the garden in "rooms" designed by Jacques Couëlle for one of the first villas of the Aga Khan in Porto Cervo. All the senses must be satisfied: the steps to walk more easily through the garden, the scents of the Mediterranean vegetation for the sense of smell, the flowers of the hibiscus and marigolds for their brilliant colours. The sculptures set in the garden are by Marisa Lambertini.

*On the left a detail of a garden in Porto Rotondo
designed by Pietro Porcinai. The Mediterranean vegetation has been respected in its
naturalness, enriched only by the flowers which blossom in thick clumps near
the house, then gradually giving way to the greenery. Below the garden designed by
Sgaravatti Mediterranea with hedges screening the sea view.*

On these two pages another two garden designs by Gamondi
and Antonioli and by Sgaravatti Mediterranea. _Below_ the climbing plants camouflage
the low stone building. _On the facing page_ the most exclusive holiday village on the
coast: the Country Club. The rocks have all been preserved and climbing plants and
clumps of daisies have been added to minimize their stark appearance.

In the photo below a view of a garden on the beach.
In the foreground, Lavandula spica (Lavender) and behind it the pale blue
flowers of Plumbago carpensis, a soft shrub that flowers between June and October.
On the facing page a detail of the exclusive Puntaldia holiday village, designed by
Gamondi and Antonioli with landscape gardening by Sgaravatti Mediterranea.
A particularly strong type of grass, Uganda, grows between the paving stones.

*On these two pages, above a luxuriant
garden in flower by Sgaravatti Mediterranea.
The details, from the left on the facing page in the foreground
Juniperus (Juniper), the yellow flowers are marigolds and the white ones daisies
(Chrysanthemum frutescens). In the centre red Pelargonium and Lantana Camara,
in the third photo there is American Vine (Ampelopsis veitichii) on the wall,
Hydrangea (Hidrangea macrophylla) and Daisies (Chysanthemum frutescens).
The shrub is a Phillyrea augustifolia, a Mediterranean plant with leaves
resembling those of the olive tree. The detail on this page
shows the house covered with Bougainvillaea glabra,
which is fond of the sun and heat but
also requires a lot of water.*

On the facing page another detail of
the garden designed by Jacques Couëlle, with hydrangea
(Hidrangea macrophylla) in the foreground. It grows well under the trees
because it likes the shade and damp soil. In the photo below a detail of a garden
in Romazzino looking on to the sea, designed by Gérard Béthoux
and landscaped by Sgaravatti Mediterranea.

*On the facing page a very refined small dwelling
designed by Luigi Vietti on the beach of the "Sweet Bride" in Porto Cervo.
The border is Verbena and Lantana Sellowiana, a plant which grows like a carpet
and flowers for a very long period. Below another detail of the garden by Pietro
Porcinai with an irregularly shaped pool and the sea
of Porto Rotondo in the background.*

Outdoor rooms

ALFRESCO LIVING was originally to celebrate the fine weather, and here these areas have been created with the greatest of care. Adjacent to the villas, these are real outdoor rooms, the majority of which increase the living space available. In part because of current building regulations and in part thanks to the creativity of the architects, they stimulate the designers to conceive them as well organized to double

the living area. We can see solutions which repeat the dining area next to the kitchen complete with a magnificent barbecue. A lounge next to the pool. At other times, due to the bizarre lie of the land, pavilions are created to welcome guests in the middle of the lawn. Sofas made of masonry under the shelter of a cane covering let the sea view be enjoyed until the sunset and even afterwards. All the designs are the offspring of this wild nature and tame it or are dominated by it.

The lounge on the sea <u>below</u> is in the garden of a villa in Punta Volpe. The seating is made of mosaic-covered cement and the table is made of a thick slab of granite.

In the large photo, the raised
terrace with a barbecue area of a small house,
Gérard Béthoux's renovation of a typical Gallura-style shepherd's shelter in San Pantaleo,
at the foot of beautiful mountains. The hand-made granite sink, the antique juniper bench,
the antique Kilim and oriental cushions are from the antique dealer Silvio Cattarinich who works in Palau.
In the photos on the facing page two details of the outdoor lounge and dining area with a north-western
exposure of one of the first villas built just ten minutes away from Porto Rotondo in a quiet
area with a view of the whole bay, closed on the east by the isle of Mortorio.
The original design was by the architect Leonardo Fiore, but alterations
have since been made including the terrace overlooking
the sea, shown on the previous pages.

An interesting solution by the designer Vanni Fiori.
This is the renovation of an apartment located in a three-family villa on the bay of Porto Cervo.
The owners wanted mainly to get more enjoyment out of the living area and
the covered terrace, as well of the garden.
The design limits, due to current legislation which is very strict on increasing volumes,
acted as an incentive for an original solution.
The garden to the south, facing the sea, has been enhanced by the local granite steps in an amphitheatre arrangement,
eliminating not only the difference in height but becoming a base for the large porch furnished with sofas and a table.
In addition, the covered terrace has been enhanced by creating a conversation
area covered by a wood and cane bower similar to the one below.

On this page and on the facing page above a room
in the open, by the Gamondi-Antonioli Studio, in a very green
part of the Costa Smeralda. This area, which acts as a barbecue
and alfresco dining room, is enclosed by a wall which is entirely faced
by Sardinian stone on the outside whilst the internal side is sheer white,
like the furnishings. The masonry barbecue has a rounded hood,
evocative of old Sardinian ovens and is supported by small granite
columns. *On the facing page below* a renovation by Gérard Béthoux,
in Porto Cervo Marina, next to the marina itself and the Yacht Club.
The aim was to increase the outdoor space as well as how it
communicated with the indoors and join the two parts of
the building by a patio to be used as a summer lounge.
The roof gives the sensation of being in a real room,
which is not usually the case with porches.
The load-bearing structure is made of
chestnut wood. The existing field stone
facing has been refined by "dry"
plastering in the joints using
coloured paste plaster.

On the facing page barbecue and lunch on the old stones,
where the owners have had stools and tables carved out of the granite not to ruin
the natural effect of the rocks. Porto Rotondo is behind us and we are facing Porto Cervo.
All the objects come from *"Casa e Cose l'Arredamento P.R."*, the shop in the small square of
Porto Rotondo. *On this page*, *above* a barbecue by Gamondi and Antonioli in the
Country Club which takes advantage of a natural situation. The barbecue
has a natural hood in the crevices of the rock. Below the barbecue of the
"Stazzu" Club. A private club has been opened in this typical
shepherds' construction, behind Porto Rotondo, where
the most typical Sardinian dish, spit-roast *"porceddu"*
or suckling pig, can be enjoyed.

"This is a house with a circular plan around a patio which can be used like a terrace overlooking the sea". These are the words of the architect Cini Boeri who also chose the location for this villa in La Maddalena, in Abbatoggia, imagining a building inserted into the rocks and facing the sea. The patio acts as a link between the three guest rooms (in the north-western arch) and the main body of the house. The architect wanted the house to blend in with the surrounding nature, a nature made of sculpted rocks hewn by the winds and the sea, typical of that part of Sardinia. The plaster of the house has been obtained by crumbling the granite of the rocks. "This meant having the same colour as the granite surrounding the house in all lights, with the rain and with the sun". White cement has been used for the patio and for the terrace above which thus gives a white edging to the upper contour of the curves of the walls.

A real
living room designed
by Gianfranco Orecchia
near the main villa,
in a garden full of olive trees,
tamarisks, juniper and
bougainvillaea,
which lies on the promontory
of Monte Ladu, dominating the view
of the bay of Cugnana from a height
of about 100 metres above sea level.
The traditional Sardinian style
roof is given movement by three pitches
which are interlocking and in part
rest on the rock of the mountain
and in part are supported by the
load-bearing structure of chestnut beams.
Old tiles have been used for the facing
above with canes underneath
to obtain an even more rustic effect.
The cupboard doors, the stools and the table
which reproduces a windrose
using tiles by Cerasarda,
are made of pinewood.

In the photo above the porch
which is part of the renovation by Gérard Béthoux
of a villa in the marina of Porto Cervo. The handmade terracotta floor
tiles by "Ceramica Diemme" are very interesting while the bench and table are covered with
brush-painted ceramic tiles. The effect of great brightness has been played on here using warm
and intimate colours. _On the facing page_ a very inviting veranda designed
by Vanni Fiori for a villa in the Pevero Golf Course area.
The furniture is from Arredare, the Milan-based shop which
also works in Sardinia with its staff of interior decorators.
The table and chairs are covered with a "rural"
patchwork fabric which is very
cool and pleasant.

We are at Punta Lada near
Porto Rotondo and in this villa the gracious
hospitality of Sardinia, its flavours and colours can
be enjoyed. The mistress of the house, Marella Giovannelli,
is from Gallura and offers us some local specialities: "Rau" jams
and preserves, "Mancini" and "Monti" wines, and bread from
the "De Rosas" bakery. The tables are laid with plates and
tablecloths from the "I.S.O.L.A." chain of Sardinian
shops, almost the island's ambassador in the
main towns. The villa was originally designed
by the Gamondi-Antonioli Studio for the
actress Claudia Cardinale.

On this page
an original solution with a rational flair
for the relaxation corner near the pool. This is a very good
choice as the pool is not very close to the house as usual
but is tucked between the rocks of Porto Rafael.
The design is by the architect Marina
Perrot of the Acquamarina studio
in La Maddalena. *On the right*
a detail of the dining area.

Above a rarity:
the porch of the only house in Porto Rotondo
which has been there since 1920. It is the home of a
Sardinian couple who are very proud of this heritage and
have been able to keep everything as it was sixty years ago.
On the left the outdoor cooking area. As well as
the grill for meat, there is also the oven for
bread but also for succulent delicacies
cooked in earthenware pots.

179

<u>On these two pages</u>
the porch bounding the apartment in the
"La Dolce Sposa" residential complex located on the tongue
of land which encloses the natural harbour from the sea and with
a panoramic view of the Marina of Porto Cervo. The renovation of the
interior was done by Gérard Béthoux. The arch motive with the decorative
function of framing the view is recurrent giving the interior rhythm.
The outdoor lounge is divided into a sitting room area, <u>above</u>,
with outdoor wicker furniture made by local craftsmen.
<u>On the facing page</u> the other arch with the
dining area. The custom-made table
is made of Spanish marble and
terracotta. The iron chairs add
a pretty touch. The floor
is made of scratched
Orosei marble.

In the photos above from the left the dining area, on a covered terrace,
directly communicating with the kitchen. *Next to it* a porch for this villa in Piccolo Romazzino with a romantic
atmosphere thanks to the large bougainvillaea. *Above on the facing page* the terrace with the masonry seating.
Cushions covered in thick yellow and white striped sail canvas.
On the right the barbecue of the first design by the
architect Rigatuso in Porto Rafael.

In the photo below the barbecue on the terrace designed by Gamondi and
Antonioli at the Country Club. This exclusive holiday village, perched on a sheer hilltop 300 metres
above sea level and with a priceless view of the harbour has this observatory of no fewer than 50 square metres.
Everything here has been designed and made by local craftsmen. The wall structures are faced with
granite stones and the load bearing beam of the roof
rests on the large rock.

The Pools

SWEET WATERS. Whether they stretch out to become an integral part of the sea on the horizon, or whether they are hidden amidst rocks and vegetation, the swimming pools on the Costa Smeralda are special. They are all out of the ordinary and, depending on the imagination of the architect, they become a low and irregularly shaped pool like the one where Narcissus gazed at his own reflection, or they are liquid mirrors in which the villas are reflected day and night in a spectacular duality. Set apart and with less ostentation, other pools give a raison d'être to secluded areas, complete with everything necessary for dining or outdoor relaxation, with a sensation of coolness and well-being.

*In the photo above the almost circular
pool designed by Gianni Gamondi with Vittorio Antonioli,
which merges into the blue of the sea. The islands of Molara and Tavolara
can be seen in the background. On the facing page a hydromassage
effect ruffles the waters of a large pool designed by Vanni Fiori, who
also designed the pool on the following pages in Romazzino,
completing the restoration of a house by Luigi Vietti.*

*In the photo above the pool built by the Gamondi-Antonioli Studio
at the Country Club, taking advantage of a natural pool. On the facing page above a shallow
pool designed by Jacques Couëlle decorated with Biot ceramic tiles. In the centre the swimming
pool open to the public at the Country Club designed by Gamondi-Antonioli which
has safeguarded nature. Below designed by Gérard Béthoux, granite boulders
forming a cascade have cleverly been brought to this pool.*

188

In the small photos on the right two details of the same pool
designed by Béthoux and Careddu. Towards the sea, there is an overflow
channel decorated with a polychromatic mosaic and looking towards the mountains
a small cascade amidst the rocks. *Below* a pool designed by Jean Paul De Marchi
on the hilltop of Monte Ladu, tucked between the rocks. In a very cool spot,
it is made completely of granite and has a panoramic view
of both the lagoon of Cugnana and of the bay
of Porto Rotondo.

Above the pool
of one of the villas designed
by Luigi Vietti for a complex
that the architect thought was for
a less affluent public than his first
clients. Built during the 1970s,
they are beautiful and chic like
all this designs and are called
the "Romazzine". *Below*
a rectangular pool painted
white to reflect the water's
transparency, it fits in perfectly
with the green vegetation.
It is in the home of Gianni
Gamondi and his wife Lalla,
an interior decorator, who
designed the furnishings
for the whole house in
the same shades
of light blue.

On these pages a breathtaking pool designed by
Gérard Béthoux looks on to the sea of Romazzino. On the following pages an
evocative solution by the landscape architect Porcinai in collaboration
with the architect Bozzalla. They have transformed
the patio into a pond in harmony
with the architecture of the
Gamondi-Antonioli Studio.

On this page, *above* a swimming pool with a granite edge
and terracotta tile flooring and, in the background, the large outdoor lounge
with a particularly "wild" roofing. The same architect, Gérard Béthoux,
also designed the spectacular solution in Porto Rafael *on the facing page*.
Its undulating shape can be seen and, in the background,
the water lapping the artificial granite beach.

The elements of the Costa Smeralda style

We are almost at the end of this book of examples but also of atmospheres, rich but also simple elements which evoke a centuries-old memory. The "material" culture of these places. Gallura and especially its coast where we have lingered is the north-western part of Sardinia, historically with a small population, without large settlements but with the traditional "stazzus" where the shepherds sheltered, although the name better refers to the enclosures, like the farms or the groups of farms. A very simple and poor architecture from which, as we have seen, all those who have worked here have tried to transfer its spirit but not the small dimensions, into their buildings. Between the client and the architects there has always been a certain complicity due to the difficult and wild nature of the place which people either love or hate. When this nature is loved, it almost "orders" the way of building, with an approach to certain elements which become a style because they form a common language. The rustic nature of the external walls, of the corners which very often are deliberately not at right angles, the rustic plasters, at times mixed with crushed granite and natural pigments which fade with time. The skilful work in some wooden objects, without a finish but left raw to change as the seasons come and go and years pass. The old roof tiles not to alter the overall natural appearance; granite which dominates; floors, walls, doors and window frames and ceilings must form a suitable frame for the furniture, the fabrics and accessories, which are not at all pretentious but very simple. Even if the place is magical and devoted to the holidays of a lucky few, the elements making up these houses are deliberately not overdone, but apparently natural and even slightly time-worn. Here, the credible patina of time gives greater chic, as if the traces of princes and aristocrats who were the first to settle on the Costa Smeralda in the wake of Karim Aga Khan marked out a path to follow, not one of ostentation but respectful of the enchanting nature which in the early 1960s was still intact. The Costa Smeralda style is a living style, there are no real rules but a series of ideas, a world to be taken as an example and to imitate. In this chapter we will only reveal the most exclusive tricks that the architects, skilfully helped by local workmen and craftsmen have successfully used in creating their fascinating interiors and exteriors. To simplify reading, we have divided the chapter into sub-chapters: interior decoration and crafts, architectural details, floors and ceilings. This will be followed at the end by information on these creators, from the building firm to the individual stone-cutter, from the most exclusive large craft ceramics supplier to the most evocative interior decorator.

<u>On the left</u> the trick here is in the "soft" walls obtained using a structure of soft iron, "nervometal", which is moulded and then plastered. Like a stage set, the design comes to life not only on paper but also in reality.

Interior decoration and crafts

It is difficult to summarize years of taste and the exchange of ideas between all those whose work appears in this chapter. In six pages our aim has been to emphasize the love for collections that immediately make a house a home, even if it is lived in for only a few months each year. It is also the skill of each individual craftsman working with wood or wrought iron, in these first two pages, to continue with hand-woven fabrics and to finish with ceramics. A way of saying that if the villas have been built recently, their interior decoration has the craft flavour not only of Sardinia but sometimes of the south of Italy or Tuscany, not to mention the Mediterranean as a whole, an endless source of ideas and evocations. The perfection of the craftsmanship, a unique and unrepeatable style which is fully expressed here and which the whole world envies, with our small craft businesses of "beautiful workmanship" which we can call "art".

In Luigi Vietti's villas, collections are compulsory.
Here his antique sailing ships are displayed on the wall of the lounge.
Sardinian woven fabric is used for the cushions on the step and on the stools.
As well as for himself, the great architect liked to show his clients Sardinian crafts
and would guide them so that they too became
connoisseurs and collectors.

*<u>Above from the left</u> a wrought
iron gate in a villa by Vanni Fiori; <u>in the centre</u>
a niche by Béthoux designed to enhance a piece of furniture.
<u>On the right</u> a 1700 wrought iron bed. <u>Below from the left</u> a door carved by the craftsman Savigni
according to the tradition handed down in his family, <u>in the centre</u> a craft-made polychromatic piece
of furniture in antique style, <u>on the right</u> in a house by Béthoux, the built-in wardrobe
doors with soft wood panels and lozenge-shaped fretwork, for the circulation
of the air, common to the architects working
on the Costa Smeralda.*

<u>On this page</u> a choice of Mastro Raphael
craft fabrics, with different weaves in tones of ecru and white.
The embroidery on the cushions is of naturalistic and marine inspiration.
In Vanni Fiori's lounge can again be seen the lozenge pattern incorporating
a light for a rhythmic background on the ceiling.

<u>Above left</u> the four-poster bed,
very much used in the beautiful bedrooms of the villas we have photographed.
<u>In the small photographs above</u> a tablecloth/cover with elaborate central embroidery
made by a local craftswoman on Vietti's instructions like the beautiful and
gaily coloured cushions <u>in the small photo below right</u>.

The crockery laid on the table <u>in the photo above</u> is by Cerasarda,
as are the floor and wall tiles of the kitchen <u>below</u>. This is in a house by Vietti,
from the first period of this production created specially for the Aga Khan with the artistic help of
Jacques Couëlle based on his experience in Provence. The ceramic sphere is the
work of the artist Pignatelli and was commissioned to enhance a path
in a house by Gamondi and Antonioli on Punta Lada.

Above a detail of ceramics
by a craftsman from Siniscola in the rustic home of the architect Paul-Auguste Gilliot.
It is also worthwhile recalling that the Petra Sarda production in San Pantaleo was created by a
farsighted lady to offer once again a type of ceramics that had always existed in Sardinia.
Below left a collection of corals and seashells on a small table, *in the centre*
a "wedding" vase typical of Cagliari which is used as an "examination piece"
by those specializing in artistic ceramics (work by the ceramist
Assemini). *On the right* a collection
of crafted tankards.

Architectural details

The flavour of the houses can be reduced to a few simple rules. In the first place, granite, which as we have seen, exists as a "field boulder" and in hewn blocks or slabs (as in the detail in the centre). Granite has always been a precious commodity and it has its connoisseurs. Here all architects, after they have designed the walls they want in stone, have to consult an expert to choose the stones to use. Centuries of dry stone walls to enclose land, protect the animals or build their own houses are in the eyes of these Sardinians who know

how much nature has worked for them, rounding the corners, bringing out colours and veins. All this has to be brought out to the very best, it is a "capital" that is to be spent intelligently and they know how to get the most out of it. Finely crushed granite is used together with natural pigments to make coloured plaster which is then always unevenly. Lastly, canes which were once supported by juniper beams, now a real luxury which no-one can afford, have been replaced by chestnut wood or woods from other regions.

*Above the small window on to the sea
is emphasized by quarry stone that has been hewn whilst the rest
of the walls are made of field stones. On the facing page from the left a
Portuguese tile in the plaster of a house, in the centre small handmade Biot tiles
for the bathroom. The lozenge-shaped tiles in the outdoor shower are by Diemme,
with their colours inspired by the transparency of the sea.
In the centre from the left a bathroom with stone chips, in the centre
a bird painted in oil on the frame of a window,
on the right a porch with a dry stone wall and cane
roof supported by chestnut wood beams. Below left a multiform
corner by Béthoux, in the centre a small front door, on the right a grit
and crushed pottery plaster edged with
a white ceramic zig-zag design.*

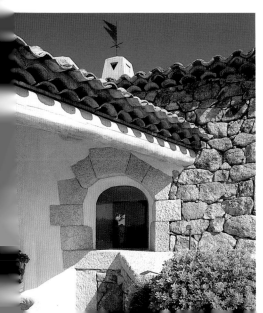

On the left, _this page_
a minimalist staircase by Béthoux
to reach the mezzanine. The idea
was inspired by the staircase by Carlo Scarpa
in the Castelvecchio Museum, Verona.
On the facing page from the top
the first five photos are details
in the houses designed by Béthoux
which propose the same materials
used for different types of solutions.
In the centre on the right
a detail of a kitchen in the restoration
of a villa by Vietti. _Below from the left_
a stairwell, a bathroom and a staircase.

Choosing the floors

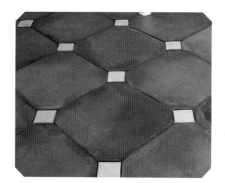

Since their beginnings in the Middle Ages as beaten earth floors covered by reeds and straw, floors on the Costa Smeralda remained the same over the centuries in the simple shepherds' shelters but have now become one more opportunity to display a sophisticated decoration which always bears in mind the aspect between country and sea, typical of this part of Sardinia. And so we shall see terracotta tiles of varying sizes, strictly handmade as in the olden times. When the tiles are glazed, the clay can still be seen underneath. But wood is also very popular, from the highly classical teak, which evokes the decks of the boats many owners and architects consider their real second home, to granite, this time from quarries and dressed, used alone or inlaid with wood.

When the architects are lucky enough to find old floors during renovation, these are usually salvaged and, after being waterproofed, are laid again. There are still some manufacturers, mostly in Italy but also in France and in Spain, that produce terracotta and glazed tiles using craft methods and so replacement is all the easier.

On the facing page, *above* and *left* terracotta
tiles with majolica insets. *On the right*, Biot tiles commissioned
in various sizes by Jacques Couëlle for his house on Monte Mannu. *Above* three examples from houses by Béthoux,
on the left and *on the right* with different shapes of natural or white glazed transparent and opaque terracotta tiles. *In the centre*
the floor and wall tiles are designed on a scale of 1:20 and specially produced. *Below* the exterior of Krizia's villa
by Gianni Gamondi. The floor is made of solid teak 3 cms. thick left natural and fixed with wooden
nails between the thick slabs of quarry granite.

Personalizing ceilings

Ceilings in Sardinia are finished in a great variety of ways from the elaborate, with smooth whitewashed plaster on unfinished surfaces which, more simply, are the visible part of the structure bearing the roof or the floor above, to open canes. Open beams or structural beams should be left in as natural a state as possible. If damaged parts have to be replaced or made from scratch, it is always better to use salvaged material. Very often the ceiling is overlooked when giving the room its overall appearance but in these houses it is an essential element in creating that effect of warmth and harmony which is found in the majority of the villas. The Costa Smeralda style is also the evocation of the humble crafts of peasants and farmers and is characterized by the slightly imperfect work of men who built their homes by themselves or with a few neighbours using simple tools and materials found locally.

On this page above
a porch by Gérard Béthoux with chestnut beams painted white. To obtain a patina of time, the beams are painted white and then most of the paint is removed by rubbing a clean dry cloth against the grain. This procedure leaves a slight patination of colour on the surface and is most visible in interstices and the grain. Below left the ceiling in Krizia's house by Gamondi, Antonioli and Voigt with trusses that form a cross. This load-bearing structure emphasizes the dining area. On the facing page, large photo the renovation of a villa by Studio Delta. In the centre, in the small photo the detail of the metal joint fixing the beams in a bell shape. Above a detail of a porch by Béthoux with the patinated white beams and blue planks. Below the false ceiling with canes supported by juniper beams in a former shepherd's shelter in Porto Cervo.

The creative minds: who and where

ARCHITECTS

Studio Vietti

Luigi Vietti's drawing, design, photograph and documentation archives have been donated by his heirs to the CSAC (University of Parma).

Manager: Dr. Gloria Bianchino
Location: Parma - Opening hours: 9-13 / 15-17
Tel. 0521 270847 - Fax 0521 270832
E-mail: csac@ipruniv.cce.unipr.it

Studio Gamondi

Gianni Gamondi is flanked in his Arch. In. S.a.s. by V. Voigt, by the architects E. Ortiz, C.L. Gariboldi, Annalisa Pitonzo, Paola Guenzi and by the geometers Paolo Salis, Marco Buttafava and by the technicians A. Gherardini, M. Coralli, C. Bignami and Elisa Gamondi.

Proprietor: Gianni Gamondi
Location: Milan - Porto Rotondo (SS) - St. John's (Antigua)
Tel. 02 67078209 - Fax 02 67078327
E-mail: arch.gamondi@arch-in.it
E-mail: emerald@candw.ag

Studio Béthoux

Craftsmanship is everything in Gérard Béthoux's office, where Mario Saba, architect, also works.

Proprietor: Gérard Béthoux
Location: San Pantaleo di Olbia
Tel. 0789 65344 - Fax 0789 65354
E-mail: bethouxg@tin.it

Studio Busiri Vici

The current proprietor of this Rome-based office, Giancarlo Busiri Vici, treads in the footsteps of his father Michele, who himself continued a tradition of architects in the family for thirteen generations.

Proprietor: Giancarlo Busiri Vici
Location: Rome
Tel. 06 8840658 - Fax 06 8543795
E-mail: giancarlobusirivici@tiscali.it

Studio Fagnola

Although Ferdinando Fagnola has several members of staff in his architectural office, the work in Sardinia is all his own.

Proprietor: Ferdinando Fagnola
Location: Turin
Tel. 011 8190714 - Fax 011 8130161
E-mail: socoarch@icsnet.it

Studio Vanni Fiori

After a 25 year stint running the Studio Vietti in Porto Cervo, Vanni Fiori is now flanked in his own office by Fiorella Fiori, Paolo Liberti, Angelo Pileri and the architect Annalisa Gulino.

Proprietor: Vanni Fiori
Location: Olbia, Sassari
Tel. 0789 58691 - Fax 0789 58491
E-mail: svfol@tiscalinet.it

Studio Acquamarina

Acquamarina and its proprietor, the architect Marina Perrot, cover their base on the island of La Maddalena and the nearby Costa Smeralda.

Proprietor: Marina Perrot
Location: La Maddalena, Sassari
Tel. / Fax 0789 737610

Studio De Marchi

The "Studio International d'Architettura e Urbanistica" has been working in the Costa Smeralda since the first Master Plan in 1963-64 and has recently moved from Porto Cervo to San Pantaleo. In addition to its proprietor, the architect Jean-Paul De Marchis, the staff now numbers Sonia Atzei, Andrea Orrù and Marco Trivellin, architect.

Proprietor: Jean-Paul De Marchis
Location: S. Pantaleo di Olbia (SS)
Tel. 0789 65429 - Fax 0789 65499
E-mail: demarchitetto@tiscali.it

Vittoria Voigt

Architecture holds no secrets for this lad of German origin. She has worked for twenty years with the architect Gianni Gamondi on the design of both interiors and exteriors. Her work consists not only of making a "fair copy" of the ideas of the architect she works with, but a lot more. "Creativity is obviously a determining factor", she tells us, "but you have to have the ability to mediate between your instinct and technical detail to make a design feasible". She takes a job "in hand" from the very start of the design, developing it and illustrating it with the various techniques suitable for each step, from a sketch to a water colour drawing. Her work can be seen on these pages and is the result of the collaboration between her imagination and "golden touch" in collaboration with Gianni Gamondi. Drawings from advanced stages can be seen here but all the many steps are stimulating. There is a first sketch which is followed by the second step, a more detailed drawing, which takes the details into consideration. "I get more satisfaction in my work through experiencing all the steps of the design up to its material completion. I have been able to gain this type of experience through having been given the greatest liberty by Mr. Gamondi with whom I work".
To the question of whether she prefers working with the design "on a large scale" or "on a small scale", her answer is easy. "I like working on the "medium" and "small" scale", she tells us, "which for me enhance the "large-scale". She does not like using computers because she considers them insufficient.
Her graphic expression of the idea behind the deign, with accurate but also romantic sensitivity, succeeds in giving the client and the builders the "flavour" of the finished work.

Vittoria Voigt
Place: Milan
Tel. 02 67078209 - Fax 02 67078327

BUILDERS

Cala Costruzioni S.r.l.
Renovation

The owner of this company has been in the trade with the organization of his company, because it is a "real" company, for twenty-seven years.
Three people work in the office in Porto Cervo and from seven up to a maximum of thirty people work on the various sites. Cala Costruzioni has a so-called "accordion" structure which is used according to real needs.
As well as training its own workmen, the company also uses other highly specialized firms: builders, joiners, installers, electricians, plumbers, technicians for alarm systems via cable or radio frequency and for satellite TV systems.
Their main activity is to salvage and readapt existing structures, they follow technical courses on materials and how to lay them and they gather documentation from qualified technicians at their suppliers, in order to be able to guarantee their work according to the specific issues that arise. The owner says, "We are proud that we can consider ourselves one of the really "ultra-specialized" firms operating on the Costa Smeralda in the specific sector of renovation".

"We have a lot of problems to cope with: dampness, condensation, mould or poor ventilation of rooms partially below ground level. Our work, supported by the use of appropriate materials, guarantees an excellent final result.
We would like to take this opportunity to thank our clients, to whom we are grateful for their loyalty, as they have been coming to us now for decades". Large or small for Cala is not a question of dimension but in the quality and value of the finishes combined with the architectural style which distinguishes the work they do.

In charge: Bernardino Caragliu
Place: Abbiadori, Porto Cervo
Tel. 0789 96695 - Fax 0789 96689

Carta Salvatore Builders

A medium-sized business which was born with small villas and is intelligent because it is moderate.
This entrepreneur who has been in the business for twenty-five years and employs about ten people on site is not only meticulous in his attention to detail but also a specialist in concrete. He works a lot on building holiday villages but is also putting the finishing touches to the Hotel Bisaccia in Portisco - a major work.
He also works in the town of Olbia and his entrepreneurial skill can be seen not only in building but also in his renovation of public buildings, such as the five hundred square metres of schools he recently built. His instinct does the rest, and thus from being a builder he has gone on to sell what he builds. He also works with Vanni Fiori and he likes to remain with his work in Gallura.
He is fond of various techniques, masonry, reinforced concrete structures, prefabricated structures, civil and industrial buildings.
Salvatore Carta tells us: "issues of a variegated nature stimulate me and I complete them to the best of my skill and according to the wishes of the architect and the client".
As builders, they deal with large contracts (3,000 sq. m. are not a problem) but they do not disdain what is "small", with special structural works and finishes, including an individual villa with great attention to detail. One of the "beautiful" things he has built is the "I Sugheri" holiday village in Porto Istana, which is also very elegant.

In charge: Salvatore Carta
Place: Olbia
Tel. / Fax 0789 28733

Costa S.r.l. and Smeralda Immobili S.a.s.

Costa deals mainly with buildings and in particular villas, whilst Smeralda Immobili looks after renovation, maintenance and outdoor work.
Everything is in the hands of a single entrepreneur, Martino Azara.
He is also the man of hidden installations, which he personally follows. He works well with Vanni Fiori for the meticulous attention to technical detail which always results in him being praised as "very good".
The building department of Costa built the last house designed by Vietti, with Vanni Fiori as manager of works.
His structure is very well organized; there are two people in the office: a surveyor and a secretary; thirteen people on site, including a surveyor here too and ten workmen with two foremen. As well as being meticulous in his work, Martino Azara is also always ready to help his clients.
"For a builder", he tells us, "it is important to follow the creativity of the architect with the most appropriate technical methodology".
Within the scope of his specialization, Azara likes building villas and in particular swimming pools, in which he is well specialized and the renovation of buildings. His firm uses new techniques and is always to the fore in the equipment it uses and its specialized labour force. "Our pride", Martino Azara continues, "is in realizing each constructive detail that the architect proposes. Our firm likes dealing with what is "small" and by small I mean work of such a dimension that our organization can follow everything directly and satisfy the client in the best and most accurate way possible".

In charge: Martino Azara
Place: Monticanaglia, Arzachena
Tel. / Fax 0789 98928

Co.M.ED. S.n.c.

They are second generation entrepreneurs. The owner, Mr. Guerri, a trained surveyor, tells us that his firm has been operating for about thirteen years with about fifteen permanent employees as well as some external firms with whom they have collaborated for a number of years.
The most important and delicate work is carried out by their qualified personnel. Naturally, Guerri takes greatest pride in the work which is particularly rich in architectural details of great value.
The various special techniques required by each building are sources of great satisfaction in his work.
"Succeeding in translating into real things what architects study on paper, trying to interpret their expectations.
At times this is complicated seeing the genius and imagination of some of them".
The architect Gianni Gamondi tells us that this is a young firm and that making beautiful houses is very important to them.
They are also admirable in the speed with which they complete the work. When asked, "Do you prefer working on large or small jobs?", the answer is: "it does not make any difference to us: because not always dimension goes hand in hand with quality". The firm is family-run and medium-sized and therefore the ambition to do their best corresponds with the ability to organize and prepare everything so that they can always complete their work within the scheduled time.
Here, as wherever building is complicated by an impervious nature, the site is more important than elsewhere. It is precisely for this reason that those who know their own land best and have been in the trade for years, learning it not at school but "on the job" are the most competent and reliable people that clients or, on their behalf,

architects, dream of having.
In Sardinia, the art of "knowing how to" is a truly ancient art; as we have had the opportunity of seeing, the island is a real "open-air museum" with its entrancing and very beautiful archaeological finds. But the way of choosing stones, of skilfully matching them, of making arches and door- and window-frames has been for years the monopoly of shepherds taking their herds seawards to graze.
The vocation of the Sardinian stone par excellence, granite, is family homes. The flavour of the rustic plasters with their natural pigments also comes from the earth and from crushed granite. Traditional elements which together with contemporary design create something "unique".

In charge: Luigi Guerri
Place: Olbia
Tel. / Fax 0789 24596

For example, as Vanni Fiori, who has worked very often with the Impresa Del Giudice tells us, "if you want arches, he knows which artisan to contact and, above all, he knows that you always need the same "touch".
One of his specialities is swimming pools and here on the Costa, you know that there are a lot of very fine and well built ones, so competition is stiff.
What's more, adds Fiori, "this firm maintains a good economic level by bringing out the quality of the work".
This underlines the reliability and professionalism of the firm.
A true specialist when it comes to executing any plan: you give him the drawings and he looks for the best solution to produce them.

Filigheddu Costruzioni S.r.l.

This father and son have been builders for two generations now.
The father began the business thirty years ago.
Their work is good and with their medium-sized firm, they are active mainly on the Costa Smeralda, which absorbs about 80% of its volume.
"Our firm", they tell us, "can count not only on employees we have trained but also on other specialized personnel".
When we ask about the extent to which creativity and technical meticulousness count, the answer is: both.
For their activity, both conditions are essential and fundamental, because working on this "coast" and above all in close conjunction with the best architects requires technical skill and ability combined with imagination.
A continuous and essential knowledge of building details and work carried out, although in the same piece, with different techniques. This skill, with a strong creative component, has developed over the years thanks to the professional collaboration of truly excellent architects and site managers.
When we ask "What are some of the problems that you have solved and which problems, connected with your work on the Costa Smeralda, are you typically capable of solving?" there is only one definite answer.
"Everything here is difficult and the requests are of a very high technical and artistic level, but perhaps the most difficult part is the ground.
Here the villas have enchanting views, but precisely for this reason they are located in craggy spots, difficult to reach and which put our capabilities to the test.

Impresa Enzo Del Giudice

His speciality, as well as building, is renovation.
His firm has worked for the best architects on the Costa Smeralda since 1980 and he can be defined an excellent executor.
As a medium-sized firm, he can work with various artisans, always succeeding in satisfying requests.
He personally organizes the sites and, according to the architect's ideas, has the sensitivity to translate any type of work into reality, and in as best way as possible.

Asking the owner of the firm what his specialization is gives only one answer: "restructuring of all work is undoubtedly the most satisfying from the professional point of view.
It becomes a challenge.
It doesn't matter whether the quantity of work is large or small, I don't make any distinctions, what counts is getting the most out of the result, leaving aside the cost of the work".

In charge: Enzo Del Giudice
Place: S. Antonio di Gallura
Tel. / Fax 079 669160
Mobile phone: 0336 814098

As a medium-sized company we can build a villa in its entirety or do a partial renovation". Our last question is whether they have had the opportunity to work outside Sardinia and the reply is: "We have been asked on several occasions, but for the time being we have declined".

In charge: Pietro Filigheddu
Place: Abbiadori, Porto Cervo
Tel. 0789 96324 - Fax 0789 96649
E-mail: filigheddu@gallura.net

F.M. Costruzioni S.n.c. di Frontello Giuseppe & C.

Giuseppe Frontello is a truly remarkable figure. His family successfully runs an excellent fish restaurant in Porto Cervo. And so what has a building company got to do with that? A lot. Just by eating at the "Briciola" in Liscia di Vacca, with its fascinating atmosphere, you can recognize the "marks" of a good bricklayer of the old-fashioned type, the ones that love their land more than anything else and that along side masters like Vietti and the Couëlles, learnt their lessons very well... He has been an artisan of building, as he likes to define himself, since way back in 1965; there are at the most five or six employees in his firm. He only uses manpower that has followed him with enthusiasm over the years, who have "worked their way up the hard way" with him. Creativity for someone like Frontello is his daily bread, it is everything, together with the accuracy of technique in details. It is clear that this small building firm gives the best of itself in building and renovation because it can express all its enthusiasm. He says with pride: "each corner in our buildings is an interesting detail, it would take a whole book to describe them all".

Due to the very high standard of quality required, the work on the Costa Smeralda offers the necessary stimulus to sharpen his wits. "Speaking about our work here, there are very many problems, first of all having to approach each building in a different way, with different solutions". "Do you prefer working on a large or a small scale?" The answer is frank: "It's choosing what is important, but in our trade it's not always possible". A source of great satisfaction was the porch of the last villa designed by Gérard Béthoux. Frontello enjoys challenges, above all when he is given carte blanche: the porch is small but a real gem. A few beams of juniper wood, gnarled to just the right extent, with canes forming a false ceiling and tiles finishing it off. The satisfaction is almost the same as that of one of his famous guests in his restaurant when he cooks fish.

In charge: Giuseppe Frontello
Place: Liscia di Vacca, Porto Cervo
Tel. / Fax: 0789 91020

Impresa Edile Artigiana Pala Antonio

Antonio Pala is an entrepreneur sui generis; he began as a simple bricklayer in Couëlle's time. He is a small businessman with a strong creative flair which he transmits with a great deal of passion to his employees. He is able to intervene at all the stages of building a villa and solve a hundred constructive details on the spot in the first person. His company is a small building business which started over twenty years ago. Ninety per cent of his turnover comes from the Costa Smeralda. His skill, as well as doing the most difficult parts himself, lies in handing down this knowledge to the young employees he "rears" on the site.

For Antonio Pala, creativeness is essential for the good success of his work. He likes renovations best which he carries out with love. "In small jobs", he tells us, "it is easier to control the success of the work". Each article requires different techniques. Here on the Costa Smeralda the architects take on major issues in the designs they develop for their clients. But then these have to be solved on the site. This is why he has a definite answer to the question, "Do you prefer working on large or small buildings?". "Small buildings, because this is where you see the real traditional skill of our earth, which every day teaches us new ways to do things. All you need is love to understand and eyes to look". And, let us add, patience to teach the younger generation that the school continues...

In charge: Antonio Pala
Place: San Pantaleo di Olbia
Tel. 0789 65405 - Fax 0789 65401

Salaris Giuseppe Impresa Edile Artigiana and I.E.S. Costruzioni S.r.l.

"I've been in this trade for thirty years", Salaris tells us "and, with my firm, I can take on large-scale jobs. I built the Cala del Faro holiday village and the Conference Center in Porto Cervo, and the Teatro Bagaglino in Liscia di Vacca". Fundamentally his execution of the work is excellent. He can create large-scale projects or small villas with great attention to detail. He is serious and reliable. Furthermore, he uses skilled employees who are assigned to very specific jobs. Training his workers takes place in two ways, as Salaris explained: "They are trained and qualified from their youth in the firm or, depending on the cases, we use workers who are already trained".

For this entrepreneur, both creativity and technical meticulousness are essential. Within their specialization, they like to build the works with an accurate interpretation of the instructions of the best architects so that the results are always perfect because the choice of materials and the quality of the works require it.

"Our real technique", Salaris goes on to stress, "is precisely building with perfect workmanship".

The quantity in volume of the finished product is established on the basis of contractual requirements. Their work, mainly linked to building on the Costa Smeralda, is the organization of various teams of workers to carry out any building job. Their skills can be put to the construction of an individual villa or, on the same level of execution, a residential or hotel complex, such as the Residence Park Hotel in Baia Sardinia. This firm is genuinely linked to the local culture.

In charge: Giuseppe Salaris
Place: Arzachena
Tel. 0789 82300 - Fax 0789 82330

Selecta S.r.l.

This is a large firm based in San Teodoro which has also worked on the Costa Smeralda and which is now mainly working on that part of the coast, south of Olbia, where there are the large villages of Puntaldia and Coda Cavallo.

The firm is specialized in building large-scale villas, although it has gained experience with hotels and villages. Builders with excellent finishing skills, the owner Gianni Mossa is extremely kind in his relations with clients, making him unique and to be privileged.

It is difficult to know which aspect of such an expert firm to praise but,

as architect Gianni Gamondi tells us, "they can interpret the typology of granite worked with great sensitivity and the same goes for the structural and finishing wood".

Collaboration with them has given such excellent results that Gianni Gamondi plans to work with them again on the major apportionment south of Olbia, on the facing isle of Tavolara. These places of natural beauty are yet to be discovered and, especially saved, from uncontrolled and over-intensive building.

With the great experience he has acquired in urbanization (for example Porto Rotondo) and the most exclusive villages on the coast, Gianni Gamondi continuously improves his "services", the result of thirty years on the Sardinian coast as well as an enormous amount of experience gained in other parts of the world. And for both large-scale and medium-scale jobs, he places his confidence in the skill and wisdom of Giovanni Mossa. And he knows that his confidence has been placed well!

In charge: Giovanni Mossa
Place: San Teodoro, Olbia
Tel. 0784 866099 - Fax 0784 869205
Mobile phone 0347 3401201

J O I N E R S

Angelo Carugati S.n.c.

Seventy year-old Mr. Carugati is a man of great experience, very capable in his trade but also a great personal friend

of the maestro Luigi Vietti. He is a real artist of furniture who studied at the Brera Academy of Fine Arts in Milan and draws with impressive and admirable skill.

There is no detail that escapes his very accurate eye, no "volute or scroll" that he is unable to emulate. A real man of art, as he is defined by another of his architect friends, Gianni Gamondi.

He loves his work to such an extent that a Carugati product can be seen immediately because, in the first place, it is "full of love".

Not only does Mr. Carugati have a golden touch and pencil, but like every good native of Lombardy, he knows how to organize the site in a class of its own. Like all geniuses, and even at his level and venerable age, he takes the measurements and does the drawings himself.

The architects often use his final drawings to submit to the client for examination.

Angelo Carugati has produced made to measure furniture and furnishings for the past thirty-seven years.

He is assisted by his son, the architect Giusto Carugati, who also follows the sector of public furnishing. They have a staff of about twenty-five people, half of whom work in the workshops and half on assembly. They do everything, on condition that they are objects of esteem and which require, in addition to creative flair, meticulous workmanship. Nothing hurried or slipshod comes out of the workshops. Dovetail joints are still made here and knowledge of wood is so great that it becomes a friend and accomplice if used with the right grain; how it moves and if you can read it like an open book. And so there is no secret to the long success that has led them to work abroad as well.

In charge: Angelo Carugati
Place: Lomazzo, Como
Tel. 02 96370764 - Fax 02 96370025

Comiti e Langiu S.n.c.

This joinery
has 33 years' experience
and is specialized in internal
and external window and door
frames and made to measure
furniture. Piero Langiu speaks to us:
"There are seven of us in the
workshop and 90% of our work is
on the Costa Smeralda. The majority
of the employees are trained here in
the shop". The pride and merit of
their work is both the creative flair
and technical meticulousness.
Within their specialization, they can
make anything to measure, from the
sliding door or window frame to
completely furnishing a home. Each
job is worthy of esteem precisely
due to the excellent relationship
with the architect. "Every job here
on the Costa Smeralda is different
and lets us continually experiment
new techniques and solutions.
Naturally, we take greatest pride in
special jobs, we do not
like large-scale distribution".
But the utmost for this small joinery,
at least according to the architect
Gérard Béthoux, is "that they are
amongst the greatest specialists in
sliding door and window frames".
They generally work with Douglas
fir, selecting the timber that they are
to work, lot by lot. Using "striped"
Douglas fir, which is cut following
the grain, these craftsmen give the
best of themselves.
They craft both the individual piece
or the piece produced in a limited
number with the same care: from
desks made of teak or a door made
of mock antique durmast with
forged nails. They are real masters!
When asked whether they have had
the chance to work abroad, the
answer is yes. They have sent door
and window frames to different
parts of the world, to islands in the
Caribbean and even to
New Zealand.

In charge: Paolo Comiti
Place: Zona industriale su Arrasolu, Olbia
Tel. / Fax 0789 50461

Dal 1885 Falegnameria Savigni Calangianus

This joinery
has a long-standing tradition
which goes back to 1885.
They have virtually trained
the most specialized
hands in the Gallura.
The father of the present
owners died at the beginning
of the 1980s and was a very
well-known carver.
Theirs is now the
fourth generation of joiners
specializing in interior decoration
and doors and working with almost
all types of wood and they have
with them between twelve and
fifteen employees. Three work on
assembly, always accompanied by
an expert who inspects the final
product. Work on the Costa
Smeralda accounts for about thirty
per cent of the total. Their
employees have always been trained
on the shop floor: as an apprentice,
the craftsman receives professional
training until he is perfectly
"qualified".
When asked whether
creative flair is essential or
whether technical meticulousness is
more important, the answer is
precise: "A craftsman, for good
workmanship of products,
considers creativity and technique as
two important factors, and if he
works with a good architect,
then creative flair is put
at his disposal".
Their speciality are internal
doors, wardrobes and cupboards
made to special design and kitchens.
"This is a type of furniture
which gives great satisfaction",
Savigni tells us, "because the work
then stands out in a highly
significant context, in the very fine
villas where we work on the
furniture and therefore the firm's
good name is always in the
limelight. As we are a small business
that works to order and to measure,
it is difficult to numerically qualify

that finished product.
Generally speaking,
I can say that internal doors and all
the furniture takes us just over a
month's work. With the rise of the
Costa Smeralda, we now satisfy
clients from many different Italian
regions and a number of European
countries with different
requirements and from different
cultural backgrounds, but with the
help of the architects, and in
particular Gérard Béthoux, we have
never had any major problems.
On the contrary, if we had some
difficulty, it was at the beginning
with the stripping technique and
aged woods, but this has since
become a technique which has
given us great satisfaction, also
because we were the first in the
area to use it".

In charge: Mario Savigni
Place: Santa Margerita, Calangianus
Tel. 079 660470 - Fax 079 661484

Sala Luigi Di Pietro S.r.l. Falegnameria Artigianale

This is now
the third generation and the
owner is still a Sala.
You have to go back to the
1930s to see the early days of this
firm. Special furnishing, window
frames and doors designed by the
most skilful architects who have
marked the history of Milanese
design made up the production,
later to become mass-produced
in the 1950s and 60s.
Their main jobs
have included the Torre Velasca,
the Pirelli skyscraper and the
Stock Exchange building in Milan.
Gradually however,
and to satisfy the demands for
increasing quality and special
attention of contemporary designers,
Sala went back to a more
craft-like dimension.
"With us today, everything continues
according to tradition and the
"trade" is passing into the hands of
the grandsons of grandpa "Gigi".

222

The architect Gianni Gamondi met the Salas in the second generation, when they solved some very difficult problems for him.

These consisted of solutions for window frames that weighed several tons and required very high technology. They have always had a quality finish, whether modern, classic or very classic. The tradition of Lombardy and of their family are combined with the sophisticated mechanisms invented for every function!

It was their idea to use liquid crystal panes in window frames. In Sardinia, where VIPs are at home, this particular solution can transform a transparent window with a view of the sea, into an opaque séparé which is a perfect protection for privacy, at the simple touch of a button.

The Agrate Brianza workshop employs fifteen people, at least two of whom work on the assembly of the frames and made to measure furnishings. The workshop employees are trained in the company, whilst self-employed craftsmen are also used for the assembly.

When asked whether creative flair is as essential as technical meticulousness, the answer is yes: to satisfy the architects they work with who are very demanding, a good amount of creative flair applied to the most sophisticated technique is necessary.

This small business can produce both window and door frames that are unique of their kind and high quality furniture for homes of class. Their extreme flexibility allows Sala to create not only wooden window and door frames but, using other technologies, also of metal alloys.

In charge: Riccardo Sala
Place:Agrate Brianza, Milan
Tel. 039 650851/2 - Fax 039 654107

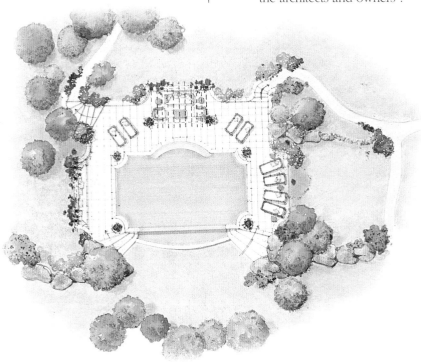

C.E.T.I.S. S.r.l.
Impresa Impianti e Piscine

According to the architect Gianni Gamondi, this is the best firm for plants and circuits on the Costa Smeralda. The training given by the owner to the employees is such that there is not only a specific and highly qualified technician to study the lighting, heating or cooling system, but also for maintenance or to build swimming pools using advanced technology. The company is also capable of offering services for lighting and irrigation maintenance in special cases, such as for golf courses.

The owner of this firm, Cesare Fenzi, has lived in Sardinia for about thirty years. A highly skilled professional, he also has an innate predisposition towards human relations. "Not only is he a scrupulously honest person", Gamondi tell us, "but he is so attentive to detail that he will study (even if

with his vast experience he would be beyond such a test) the effect of the artificial lights at night, together with the architects and owners".

He can advise the architect on the most suitable system for every need, just on the paper, for the drawn design: he decides according to the amount of energy required and uses the most appropriate technology. Cesare Fenzi takes everything into account: how the house is used and in which period or season of the year, if there are to be guests and he studies the type of system, "economic, medium-priced or very expensive only when really needed", he tells us.

Technologies are always avant-garde, from "convection" to "optic fibre" to hydromassage with "air/ozone" effects. He even purifies the water in swimming pools with "UV rays". Thanks to its dimensions, the company can also carry out the urbanization services of large allotments.

In charge: Cesare Fenzi
Place: Olbia
Tel. 0789 51409 - Fax 0789 57311
E-mail: cetis.olbia@tin.it

Cerasarda S.p.A.

Cerasarda, the famous
Ceramics of the Costa Smeralda,
started business in Olbia in 1963,
contributing with the solar colours
of its glazes and refined decorations
of its ceramics to the birth
of the Costa Smeralda legend
as a spot for dream
holidays and villas.
The work,
which has certainly become
more refined with the improvement
in techniques and investments in
highly modern machinery, still
maintains the philosophy of
a large "craft workshop" where
manual skill, with the extraordinary
care taken in finishing
each piece, is privileged.
One of the techniques that
Cerasarda has taken up again in
recent years is "hand scratching",
perhaps the oldest type of
decoration for ceramics
and majolica.
Scratching,
together with decoration,
always done by hand, gives life to
the special "decorated by hand"
pieces, almost precious parts of a
mosaic which, with the geniality of
the designers using them,
give ceramic facings of
unequalled beauty.
Porto Cervo, Cala di Volpe,
Romazzino, the hotels,
the residences and villas designed
by the most important
architects owe a great

deal to the evocations inspired
by the shapes and colours of
Cerasarda ceramics, a school of
ceramics the artistic basis of
which was given by artists
such as Robert Picault, one
of Pablo Picasso's disciples.
Manifattura Cerasarda
has always aimed at giving the
cultural traditions of Sardinia, and in
general of the Mediterranean, their
true value, both by suggesting
shapes and colours and by
identifying new ones, always
expressive of the original
"Mediterranean matrix".
Cerasarda is an integral part of the
activities connected with the
development of the Costa Smeralda
and now belongs to the
Meridiana airline.
The plant and registered offices of
the company are in Olbia, Sardinia,
with a branch and warehouse in
Fiorano Modenese - Modena, for
distribution on the domestic and
international markets.

Chairman: Dr. Marcello Bedogni
Commercial Sales Manager:
Gianni Manconi
Agent for Sardinia: Pier Luigi Manca
Place: Olbia (SS)
Tel. 0789 50151 - Fax 0789 50421
E-mail: info@cerasarda.it
www.cerasarda.it

Diemme S.r.l.

The business of this firm which has
existed for many years may be
described as artistic crafts. It was the
grandfather of the present owner,
Cesare Mori, who invented the "plates
of good memories". He produces
small quantities of tiles and is a
genuine ceramist. He studies over and
over again decorations that he finds
not only in the very large family
archives but also through research and
salvage of old material which is always
a source of inspiration.
He is as imaginative and creative as
his father and grandfather were before
him. They worked with the first
architects on the Costa Smeralda, who
were so selective as not to be satisfied
with ceramics from Provence but to

look for this company near Ascoli
Piceno where it is located.
For Luigi Vietti, Jacques Couëlle and
Gérard Béthoux, they produced
completely hand-made tiles and even
gilded tiles, so exclusive that
sometimes the mould was destroyed
after the agreed delivery. Not only
were the architects' designs, produced
with expertise and creative intuition
kept secret, but so was the material
that Cesare Mori manipulated with his
special glazes that were highly
resistant and at the same time very
transparent, creating a fine surface
film, as only he knew how, letting the
terracotta be seen below.
He plays a lot on sizes and is able to
keep the "vein" of his ancient art so
well hidden as to seem an alchemist,
giving a "halo of mystery" to the
product. Cesare Mori is so enthusiastic
that he moves like a fashionable
fashion designer for these "royal"
solutions with a deliberately
impoverished appearance, real
"shabby chic".

In charge: Cesare and Domenico Mori
Place: Porto San Giorgio, Ascoli Piceno
Tel. and Fax 0734 679252
E-mail: info@diemmeitalia.com
www.diemmeitalia.com

Siba Marmi

This is a real
works for craft marble and granite
cutting and is in Arzachena.
The founding partner, Isidoro
Scugugia, began business
thirty-three years ago.
For fifteen years, Antonio Bonu has
worked alongside him as partner
and another four people
work with him.
That makes a total of six
and with great pride they tell us:
"The people who work for us are
trained with a specific and complete
apprenticeship in our firm".
Here Sardinian marble is cut,
in particular the "Daino Perla"

type from Orosei, as well as all other foreign and domestic marbles. Their specialities are the finishes which require special care, such as facings for kitchens and bathrooms and fireplaces and flooring. They work to order for particularly refined designers and so everything must be of perfect workmanship. Sardinian granites, shaped and cut with particular care to add the finishing touch to swimming pools which here in Sardinia, in the villas we have discussed, take on increasingly whimsical shapes. The owners go on to say, "in our work quality and not quantity is important. Our greatest gratification is to fulfil the architects' ideas".

In charge: Isidoro Scugugia
Place: Arzachena, Porto Cervo
Tel. 0789 82206 - Fax 0789 82206
Mobile phone 0337 816411

Manera Tappezzeria and Trapuntificio Jolly

This shop in Milan has maintained over the years the characteristics of a "craft workshop" where the owners personally do the work with the passion and love they have handed down to their staff.
In a city famous for industrial design, "elegant upholstery" such as this has been on the market for no less than thirty-five years. Their work has always been of a very high standard and they are amongst the few still to use the rare and precious techniques of the masters of the past.
Training of employees, as the owner Gianni Manera emphasises, is in the firm, where creative flair and technical meticulousness are both very important. Of their specialization, which covers all upholstery work, the part that gives greatest satisfaction are decorations in passement and

embroidery on cushions, covers, curtains and hanging the work. "Clothing the home is an ancient art, of which unfortunately there are fewer and fewer traces Choosing appropriate trimmings as part of a job for a client is a choice that expresses taste, creative and artistic flair", says Gianni Manera.
"We only work to order, with non-standardized measurements and modules and we look for the best technique for each specific project.
All jobs are important for the Manera firm, whether they are large or small! Every commitment is important. Dealing with and solving the problems encountered on the job is a source of satisfaction for a small craft business like ours, which has the specific vocation of interpreting the requirements of the client and the architect. Besides, in homes on the Costa Smeralda, there has been the opportunity, through Lalla Gamondi, to express all their expertise with famous clients. These dream villas do not always have a simple interior decoration and, on the contrary, the owners often go there for reasons purely of public relations. It is here that the Tappezzeria Manera can follow their clients or the architects' clients. Only in the fine homes of long ago certain very pleasant rites are perpetuated and "haute couture" for the home is one of these".

In charge: Gianni Manera
Place: Milan
Tel. / Fax 02 89500527

Upholstery Benito Tramellino

There is only one real shop in Olbia for everything regarding the finishing touches of interior decoration and, in collaboration with the best known firms of architects, the splendid results can be seen

on the previous pages. Skilful inventors of solutions and not only upholsterers but also interior decorators, carpenters and above all real connoisseurs of Sardinian craft fabrics. From the hands of Benito, since 1960, and of Raffaella since 1970, the firm has expanded without ever losing sight of quality. As Raffaella herself says, they now have fifteen employees, plus their four children and themselves. Preparation takes place exclusively on their premises and only in exceptional cases do they call in specialized carpenters from outside. When asked how important technical skill is in proportion to creativity, the answer comes without the slightest hesitation: "Everything in the world of our work is creativity because we work like the tailors and dressmakers who are now called designers".
"That's it, we can be considered home designers: our professionalism is precisely that: having a style of our own which gives a hallmark to the interior decoration".
Raffaella goes on to say, "I like the relationship with clients, creating with them as far as possible and then continuing so that the Sardinian craft weavers produce what has been conceived and suggested. Benito is the technician who makes sure that the products are perfectly manufactured".
The Tramellino firm has an enormous production and is one of the few examples of self-sufficiency.
"This means that we can take on any element of the interior decoration, from the frame of a couch to the furniture, to making the cushions and upholstered furniture or the beautiful four-poster beds which, thanks in part to us, have now become very fashionable here. The finished product leaves the firm with "our trademark" and we are very proud of it.
Of course this very precise way of working at times makes it difficult for us to respect delivery schedules".

"Imagine", Raffaella continues, "that there are people here who make almost impossible demands".
For example, giving us only thirty days to deliver the interior decoration to a villa, including craft-made furniture and fabrics. We can do it because we work with great enthusiasm: the moment of truth comes when you see that the harmony you have created with the people you work with gives rise to a beautiful building".
"We have handed down this passion to our children and this means, as long as they are Tramellinis in Olbia, that we will be able to produce things of exquisite taste and excellent quality with the old techniques. We mainly work here: about 90% of our production is for the Costa Smeralda but when possible we are obviously pleased to export our style of sobriety and good taste".

In charge: Raffaella Tramellino
Place: Olbia, Porto Cervo, Firenze
Tel. 0789 51019 - Fax 0789 53240
E-mail: benito.tramellino@tin.it
www.tramellinoarredamenti.it

NURSERY AND GARDEN CENTER

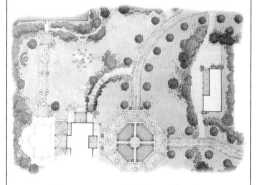

Sgaravatti Geo S.r.l.
Sgaravatti Land S.c.a.r.l.

A leader in the production of plants and landscape design, we have mentioned this name several times in the book in connection with the gardens on the Costa Smeralda and the fruitful collaboration with the well-known architects working in this area.
As Giuseppe Carteri explained

to us in an interview, Sgaravatti Mediterranea is a "point of reference" for plants in Sardinia and has been so for very many years now.
There is a large nursery in Capoterra, near Cagliari, covering 32 hectares where each year about one million ornamental plants for indoors and outdoors are grown. All the Mediterranean plants are grown and sold, from the most well-known ones to exotic, rare and medicinal species.
There are countless parks, gardens, tourist and sports complexes that have been designed and landscaped by Sgaravatti Mediterranea who also do the maintenance, using species suitable for the creation of spaces in harmony with the landscape.
The company, with its specific scientific knowledge, has been working for several years on the territory and environmental reclamation of degraded areas, with the creation of wind-breaking and anti-noise barriers.
A century and a half of business in harmony with nature. Seriousness and competitiveness, experience and a pinch of magic are the ingredients that make Sgaravatti synonymous with plants, parks and gardens. Here in Sardinia an important point is the Garden Center in Porto Cervo, on the road to Abbiadori. Expert advice can be found here with an unrivalled supply of products and services for the garden, terrace and house plants. The lawn sown with "Uganda" grass was for many years an exclusivity of Sgaravatti, as it was Benedetto Sgaravatti who brought the seeds for the first time from that country. A successful intuition for a lawn of top quality, suitable for public parks and for sports facilities.

In charge of Nursery: Rosi Zuliani Sgaravatti
Place: Capoterra (CA)
Tel. 070 728025 - Fax 070 728342
E-mail: sgamed@tin.it
In charge of Garden Centre:
Giuseppe Carteri
Place: La Punga, Arzachena (SS)
Tel. 0789 98803 - Fax 0789 98701

Arredare S.r.l.

The owners of this elegant and very well known shop in Milan are Alberto and Mauro Tambelli. They are in fact the second generation as the firm was founded by their father.
On his retirement, they wanted to continue the tradition but with a managerial spirit which is all to their credit!
They provide high level furniture, in agreement with clients and architects or interior decorators, to completely furnish a house, ready to live, in only three months.
As well as the most well-known designer names which Arredare has always distributed, they also offer a service for the clientele which includes the design and realization of "designer interiors" of quality. Mauro Tambelli tells us: "looking for harmony between shapes and colours, but also the technical aspects which have to be taken into consideration, are a privileged part of our specialization".
Nowhere as in this shop is the choice as wide and exclusive. As far as bookcases, fitted walls and upholstery are concerned, we have our own purely craft production. In the case of large-scale supplies, we are able to call on other suppliers.
Our staff of young architects and decorators can do surveys on the spot, direct the works, provide artistic supervision and advice on combinations of materials, fabrics, colours and lights, design, execution and laying and after-sales assistance.

They also co-ordinate decorators, plasterers, electricians and upholsterers. When asked whether they prefer working on a large scale or on a small scale, the answer is "in both cases the passion is the same. Large or small have a meaning only in the number of items provided, we try to be as helpful as possible with everyone".

In charge: Alberto and Mauro Tambelli
Place: Milan
Tel. 02 712514 - Fax 02 7383334
E-mail: arredare_s.r.l.@iol.it
www.arredareonline.com

Casa e Cose S.r.l.
Portorotondo

I spoke to Bibi Accarisi who has been here in Sardinia for a very long time. Born in Florence, she arrived in this part of the world after art studies, "learning" the trade from a famous aristocrat from Puglia, Duchess Fiorenza Serena di Lapigio. For the duchess, interior design is, or rather was, a mission because her age no longer allows her to fight like a "tiger". She had already taken part in the first two stages of the development of the Costa Smeralda and together they created a large shop, with all the major brand names of mass production or small crafts.
Now Bibi works with another partner, Ofelia Fiori, and they share a taste for discovery and research. The shop is the showcase of the most chic interiors in Porto Rotondo and stands right on the squall square.
As soon as you enter, you immediately feel the taste and flair of these two young ladies. "We like doing everything, says Bibi Accarisi, "from demolishing an apartment and designing it again from scratch, from the start to the end, calibrating every inch and every cent… Or choosing things that are really "in" and eye-catching for the shop. In our trade you always have to be up to date and Ofelia and I like new colours and rich fabrics that can personalize a room. For example, this year we have staked on English fabrics made in India which are really special… Both of us like objects, from English silver to ethnic ceramics. Once we sold "poor" antiques from Tuscany to Umbria, we would buy well and got good prices when we sold.
Now we collaborate on furnishing villas, including very large ones, with the architects here.
But our speciality is apartments. From 40 sq.m. to 150 sq. m. We are female interior designers but practical and we know how to cut out space in a very rational way for our clients, whom we often follow outside Sardinia, to decorate their homes in the city or the mountains!
We are eclectic: according to the budgets we mix antiques, maybe a fine wardrobe, or high-tech solutions, if the kitchen is large.
We are not particularly decorative, we use Spanish terracotta and Cerasarda tiles of a certain type. Not very much Vietri because it is very expensive. What have we got that other male interior designers don't have? Perhaps our practical sense. We tend to have the money spent on the structure: the volume, light and space.
Then the rest just comes along".
This does not mean to say that they are not able to design exclusive pieces such as the very fine wrought iron standard lamps which are to be found everywhere, including at the Hotel Cala di Volpe.

In charge: Bibi Accarisi
Place: Porto Rotondo, Olbia (SS)
Tel. 0789 34331 - Fax 0789 381401

Cose Belle di Ivana Sarotti

Its name is "Cose Belle" and it is the most fashionable furniture shop in Porto San Paolo and its owner and "author" is Ivana Sarotti. It is right in the square and is run by this dynamic blonde lady with blue eyes.
She opened it in 1987 and since then has followed it with a genuine vocation.
The name was not chosen by chance. "For me", says the owner, "pleasing my clients, who come back to me and become loyal, is the most gratifying part".
With a degree in something quite different many years ago, she moved to Sardinia and here she followed her true vocation. She began to study design and interior design very seriously and now says with pride: "I have always been creative, but in fact my work began almost by chance. First of all I built my own house, which I decided to have designed by Vanni Fiori, then I designed the interior outlay, the furniture and the furnishings and I had them craft made in Milan.
Here I work exclusively with a craftsman who is far more sophisticated than I am. Since then, whoever came to visit me asked me to create something similar for them too.
The shop completes this research of mine, emphasizes my intuitions in the field of taste, colours… For example, I was one of the first to suggest the "ethnic" look which is now very successful.
One of my passions is choosing objects and accessories at international fairs but obviously if I am not moved by an emotion I don't choose it…".
Vanni Fiori says of her: "you can say she's a perfectionist, both in the shop and as an interior designer. I always encourage her to continue".

In charge: Ivana Sarotti
Place: Porto San Paolo, Olbia (SS)
Tel. 0789 40441 - Fax 0789 40083

La Mariposa

An interior decoration
shop in the square in the
village of Puntaldia.
The lady
who invented this shop twenty
years ago is called Maria Antonia
Cebrelli but is probably
better known by everyone who
"counts" on the Costa Smeralda as
Lalla Gamondi.
Wife of the architect
Gianni Gamondi, Lalla runs her
furniture and accessory shop like a
real boutique. Here a home can be
completely furnished and made to
measure for the client.
As Lalla Gamondi says,
"The most difficult part of my work
is trying to interpret the needs of
who is to use the house,
maintaining an organic line
with the decoration plan".
Elegant, casual and above
all a great traveller, Lalla knows
Sardinia very well, the typologies of
the villas and the holiday villages
she has been furnishing for so long.
She also hunts down the curious or
"special" object which gives tone
and personality to a room. Mrs.
Gamondi continues:
"What I like most in the field
of work I have chosen and that
I have always been enthusiastic
about is the search for "particular"
materials and objects that
can characterize and
enhance my work".
There is nothing that is too
"small" to be overlooked in a
decoration plan by La Mariposa:
everything is studied down to the
last detail. "My job", Mrs. Gamondi
continues, "is to suggest the object,
the picture, the vase, the carpet,
contemporary or antique, that by
their presence, can give warmth to a
room or personality to an area.
For this reason, I do not consider,
even after years of personal
achievements, that I have "made it"
because I never tire of studying
the historical period, the production
that gave rise to the tiny

"work of art" that I then offer the
client. Because before it goes from
my hands into the client's hands,
I have to feel it is "mine" and I must
be the first to understand the
meaning it can take on in the
interior decoration that is being
undertaken".

In charge: Lalla Gamondi
Place: Puntaldia, San Teodoro
Tel. / Fax 02 67072642

Progetto Casa S.r.l.

Gianni Filigheddu
has worked with wall and floor
coverings for more than twenty
years. But he did not open his shop
until 1992. It is a two-floor building
a few hundred metres from the old
centre of Arzachena and on the road
that leads to the most visited spot in
the area: the Giants' Tomb. In his
shop you can find everything, from
wall coverings and floors to
bathroom fittings and taps.
He is a brilliant link
between the manufacturing
companies and the architect with
special requirements. In addition to
the more established companies, he
has made a considerable effort to
have a special display of handmade
ceramics with particular reference to
the craft products of the Amalfi
coast. The business is family-run
and so relations with clients are
always direct. Work on the Costa
Smeralda represents about 65% of
the total turnover.
Creative flair is important
to select products that arouse the
interest of architects and their select
clients. Furthermore, the technical
meticulousness and quality of the
products sold also have
to be guaranteed.
"What we like in our work is
looking for manufacturers,
promotion and introduction of the
product on to the local market, care
in client service, constant
co-operation with the sector's
technicians and assistance in laying
the ceramics. Careful management
of the orders at the start

of the project,
constant contact with the
craftsmen making the product
and appropriate transport from
mainland Italy are our pride which
allow us, to the great satisfaction of
our clients and of ourselves,
to annul the distance between
the production centres of
the individual products and
the location of the site".
And this skill in choosing
and circulating materials and goods
is so successful that he has orders
not only from all over Italy but also
to supply craft products
in New Zealand, Germany
and France.
This is a very
sophisticated Made in Italy
which thanks to Progetto Casa
goes out into the world
from Sardinia!

In charge: Gianni Filigheddi
Place: Arzachena (SS)
Tel. / Fax 0789 83310
E-mail: progettocasa@gallura.net

O U T D O O R   F U R N I S H I N G S

Unopiù S.p.A.

Unopiù has been marketing
quality outdoor furnishings
and décor for more than
twenty-five years.
Based on a blend of
modernised traditions, quality
and research, the company's
refined style has acquired a
consistent clientele among
those who enjoy experiencing
and using their outdoor spaces
with a touch of personal taste,
individual flair and above all
their own "art of living".

This explains why Unopiù has always focused on conveying its customers' love for their gardens, terraces and green spaces, complying coherently with its vocation of catering for the tastes and differing requirements of a clientele that, having a special appreciation for beautiful things, is not content merely to occupy its outdoor spaces, but wants to inhabit them, furnish them and surround itself with elegant, quality products.

And so it is that the most breathtaking and prestigious terraces in the cities of Italy and the rest of Europe, the finest gardens that adorn stately homes, the relaxing verandas in front of country hideaways in Tuscany, Provence or Bavaria, the solariums around the artwork swimming pools on the Costa Smeralda, the Côte d'Azur or the Balearics and of course a whole host of other fantastic locations all over the world are all graced by furnishings and structures by Unopiù, which have multiplied to provide a blueprint for everyone with a sense of timeless beauty.

The coasts of Sardinia as a whole and of the Costa Smeralda in particular have become a symbolic home for Unopiù. You need only browse through the company's catalogue to discover splendid photographs taken in these magical settings, places where the design, beauty, class and harmony of its extensive product range have made the finest showing of the quality, of the care for detail and use of materials and of the craftsmanship that are lavished on their production, generating an unqualified success as a result: the direct consequence of the strong personalities of the people who chose them.

In the years to come, Unopiù –

the leader in its field in Italy and other European countries – will continue offering everyone who wants to express their "art of living" the possibility to keep making their dreams come true.

**In charge: Massimo Saracchi
Managing Director, Unopiù S.p.A.
Soriano nel Cimino (VT)
Tel. 0761 7581 - Fax 0761 758555
www.unopiu.it**

PROPERTY MARKET

Agenzia della Costa S.r.l.

The Agenzia della Costa was established in March 1991, after the closure of the Costa Smeralda Real Estate Agency, the company that belonged to the founding group set up by his Highness Prince Karim Aga Khan, in which Giorgio Tedeschi and Vittorio Franco Valeri worked for many years. Known to everyone on the Costa as estate agents since 1972, the two are now the proprietors of the Agenzia della Costa.
With its head office in Piazzetta degli Affari, in Porto Cervo, and a branch office in Piazzetta dei Pini, in nearby Baja Sardinia, the Agenzia della Costa operates all over the Costa Smeralda, Baja Sardinia and bordering areas. The Agenzia della Costa targets a select international clientèle, for whom it is equipped to take care of every type of property deal, buying and selling villas, apartments, country houses, boat moorings, hotels and commercial establishments, as well as land.
The Agenzia della Costa is made up

of a group of individuals, whose responsibilities are divided between the sales and rental office, the administration and the secretariat.
The agency works in partnership with comparable structures located in other parts of the world, operating in English, German, French, Portuguese and Spanish.
"Intuition is one of the most important gifts for an estate agent. When working with a medium to high target, it becomes absolutely essential, as a fast analysis helps you get a quick understanding of what the client really needs, then put that into the perspective of the funds available for a purchase. While intuition is a natural gift, grey hair indicates a certain amount of professional experience."
"In our line of work, correct behaviour, honesty, transparency and a sense of responsibility are all essentials, together with an equitable, professional attitude towards the parties involved in a transaction and, as agents, the awareness that it is our function to mediate between them."
"The Agenzia della Costa aims to stand close by its clients. When selling a plot of building land, for example, we take part in the relationship that is created between the property developer and the institutions, providing assistance that ranges from the architectural design to getting planning permission, dealing with the subcontracting and monitoring the progress of work right through to handing over the finished building and even the final aspects of furnishing it and landscaping and planting the garden."
"We follow our customers through the whole time they spend on the Costa Smeralda, right up to the moment when they sell up again or rent their property out: that is why we try to give our best, by keeping our offices open all year round."

**Managers: Giorgio Tedeschi, Franco Valeri
Location: Porto Cervo (SS)
Tel. 0789 94300
Fax 0789 94560
www.agenziadellacosta.net
E-mail: info@agenziadellacosta.net**

Immobiliare F. Brunati

The Brunati real estate agency is situated in the village of Abbiadori, half way between Cala di Volpe and Porto Cervo. Thirty years of hands-on experience working on the Costa Smeralda is the ingredient that qualifies our work. Our knowledge of the history of the entire Costa's development combines with our personal acquaintance with the leading architects who have applied their skills to achieving the harmonious development of this quite extraordinary area, giving us the ability to put a precise value on the investments and real estate that we offer to our clients. We are perfectly aware of the fact that, when a client entertains the idea of buying a high profile property on the Costa Smeralda, the aspect of emotions can play a decisive rôle: so decisive as to influence the aspect of sound financial sense. We have what it takes to ensure that our clients are always directed towards the best investments. We like to establish spontaneous, sincere relations with our clients, because we believe that human contacts are crucial to building the trust we need. And that trust goes hand in hand with our intimate knowledge of the places and structures to shape the decision to make the right investment that corresponds to your expectations. We sell and rent prestigious villas and apartments, investing our professionalism in taking care of all the legal and administrative aspects related to property deals and partnering with the best local notaries, attorneys and accountants. We like to feel that we are part of each successful deal: we get a sense of fulfilment from our work, apply the same commitment to every investment, however large or small, and enjoy suggesting the structural improvements that can help increase its value.

Manager: Fernanda Brunati
Location: Abbiadori, Porto Cervo (SS)
Tel. 0789 96541 - Fax 0789 96534
www.costasmeraldaagency.com
E-mail: immbrunati@tiscalinet.it

La Bussola S.a.s.

The La Bussola real estate agency, proprietor Luisa Pirazzini Novello, is located in Piazzetta degli Ulivi, above the famous "walk" in Porto Cervo.
For more than thirty years, the dynamic proprietor has been able to take a personal interest in the progress in property development in this breathtaking corner of Sardinia.
Her remarkable personality, combined with her competence and professionalism, have made the La Bussola real estate agency an important landmark for an extensive Italian and foreign clientèle wanting to make a sound investment on the Costa Smeralda. A clientèle with whom the La Bussola real estate agency can work and dialogue on the same wavelength, as all its staff is multilingual.
The properties that passes through the hands of the La Bussola real estate agency are aimed at a medium to high target: in most cases, they are villas designed by the more important architects operating on the Costa Smeralda.
"The first thing we try to establish with our clients is a relationship based on trust. Sometimes, after years have gone by, we find the same clients come back to us to buy another house when their family requirements change."

Luisa Pirazzini Novello
Piazzetta degli Ulivi
07020 Porto Cervo (SS)
Tel. 0789 92272 / 92500 - Fax 0789 92351
E-mail: info@imm-labussola.com
www.imm-labussola.com

Claudio Giuntoli Immobiliare S.r.l.

Situated in Portorotondo, on the other cape of the Gulf of Cugnana opposite Porto Cervo, the Claudio Giuntoli real estate agency has been operating since 1977 and is considered to be one of the most highly qualified on the whole Costa Smeralda. As one of the most competent property development agents operating on the Costa, its founder Claudio Giuntoli recently worked with the Italian government on property development issues.
You are from Lombardy. Why did you move to work in Portorotondo? "This place tells the story of my love affair with Sardinia: I simply couldn't move away," says Giuntoli. "We feel perfectly at home with the position we have here at the other 'pole', where everything is familiar, including the way we relate to our clients."
How do you value the market for second homes and holiday villas and villages? "This market is now reaching an economic significance that puts it on a par with the first home, but with one substantial difference, because when you come here, you are buying a second home where you can live in contact with nature, the sun and the sea, while the first home is in the place where you work. I prefer dealing with the second home sector of the market."
In your opinion, how does the future look for this stretch of the Costa in property terms? "I am certain that the Costa Smeralda has a rosy future ahead of it, because once you have tried coming here to live you find that you have approached the nature of the Mediterranean, with its sea and its sun, and you will never abandon it again." "We offer long-term property investments in Portorotondo, in Porto Cervo, in Portisco, in Porto Rafael and in other places in Sardinia. We sell villas that are often the creations of truly talented architects, such as Gamondi, Couëlle and all the others. That is just one more reason why our motto says that a purchase or a sale is only good if it is a good deal for both the buyer and the seller … and that is why you need good architects."
Giuntoli is assisted in his agency by Consuelo Davoli and other highly professional staff.

Manager: Claudio Giuntoli
Location: Portorotondo, Olbia (SS)
Tel. 0789 34143 / 34351 - Fax 0789 35361
E-mail: clgiunt@tin.it

ACKNOWLEDGEMENTS

Carrying out a new editorial project and putting it on to the market requires the talents of many people and we could never have completed this book on our own; we would like to thank everybody. If unintentionally we have not mentioned someone we apologise and thank them nevertheless here, from the bottom of our hearts. In particular, for having followed us from the idea of the book up to its conclusion, we thank the beloved Kristine Beeckman, who at every moment, even at the more difficult times, was close to Giancarlo, the first creator of this volume. For his affectionate participation and acute observations, we are particularly grateful to Maurizio Piccinini who acted as art director and to Gigi Radice who, with his experience, wrote the introduction. Special thanks go to our collaborators, in particular to Laura Garzoni for her very totally responsible management of the photo archives and for her participation, Flaminia Palminteri, expert botanist, Rosaria Zucconi and Franco Marchesi, colleagues and friends and to Giuliana's nephew, Luigi Piva. For the proof-reading of the English text, thanks to David Formenti-Winchester and for their precious suggestions and corrections, special thanks go to Gérard Béthoux, Gianni Gamondi and Vanni Fiori, with the lawyer Andrea Pogliani for having taken the "court case" involving our book in Italy to heart. We also thank, for their help and enthusiasm, Giuseppe Carteri, landscape engineer, Lorenzo Enotti with Andrea Filippi and Cristina Melloni, expert photolytic and graphic artists, Valerio Rossi for his advice on the paper and Mara Filippini for having put at our disposal the best technicians of her printers Company. Above all, however, we wish to thank all those who really made these photographs possible, the people who live in and look after the houses and their gardens: they spent entire days helping and sharing in the circumstances and contingent problems with far-sightedness and without expectations, putting themselves at our entire disposal.
Messrs:
Addari, Albonico, Arduini, Asvisio, Azzena, Balestra, Battella, Berlusconi, Bonanni, Boni, Borra, Capra De Carrè, Celentano, Chiarolanza, D'Angelo, Del Pozzo, Drovetti, Deiana, Eckart, Fanfani, Franchini, Gandini, Hruska, Krieg, Lovato, Mandelli, Magaraggia, Marittimi, Marzi Giovannelli, Parodi Delfino, Partesi, Putsch, Rasero, Ronchi, Rosanna, Rossi, Sachs, Salom, Schmitz, Schneider, Seragnoli, Tossani, Uzzo, Verona.
And not last, of course, all the architects and designers with their staff.

THIS VOLUME *HOMES IN SARDINIA*
WAS PRINTED BY PUNTOGRAFICO S.P.A., BRESCIA
EUROART PAPER SUPPLIED BY
CARTARIA ITALIANA GRAPHIC PAPERS S.P.A., NOVATE MILANESE
COLOUR SEPARATION BY ALL SERVICE D.T.P. S.R.L., MILAN
BOUND BY L.E.B., BRESCIA
TRANSLATION BY COPISTERIA MANARA, MILAN
PRINTING COMPLETED ON 30TH MAY 2004

ARCHIDEOS®

LIBRI & CD
CD & LIVRES
BOOKS & CD
CD & BUCHER